1-4

Will The "Saints" Go Marching In?

Floyd McElveen

A Division of G/L Publications
Glendale, California, U.S.A.

Other good Regal reading:

What Everyone Should Know About Transcendental Meditation by Gordon R. Lewis.
So, What's the Difference? by Fritz Ridenour.
The Fortune Sellers by Gary A. Wilburn.
The Listener by H. S. Vigeveno.

Scripture quotations are from the *King James Version* of the Bible.

© Copyright 1977 by G/L Publications
All rights reserved

Published by Regal Books Division, G/L Publications
Glendale, California 91209
Printed in U.S.A.

Library of Congress Catalog Card No. 76-57036
ISBN 0-8307-0528-7

The publishers do not necessarily endorse the entire contents of all publications referred to in this book.

Contents

To my much loved and understanding wife,
Virginia McElveen;
With special thanks to Bruce and Flo Walters
and the Hoy Deeters for financial support
and prayer to keep this project alive;

To Myrna Chausse for typing and encouragement;
And to all of these for their warm love
and concern for Christ, for the author
and for our Mormon friends.

Foreword

Will you be ready when the Mormon elders knock at your door? Some years ago there was a knock at my door that was to spark an enduring interest and concern.

Two Mormon elders confronted me with Joseph Smith's claim to have restored the *only* true church on earth—all others are corrupt. They also challenged me with the teaching that I must accept Joseph Smith as Latter-day Prophet if I want to be right with God.

The challenge of those two Mormons started me on an odyssey that continues even today as more and more documents are found that relate to Joseph Smith, the founder of the Mormon religion. The search has taken me from coast to coast, into basements and attics, examining dusty writings and other relics of the past.

As I began my study of the claims of Joseph Smith, I soon discovered wide discrepancies between the original documents and present Mormon Scriptures. I met people who had abandoned their Mormon faith because Joseph Smith's claim to be a prophet, when judged by either the Bible or the Book of Mormon, was clearly in error. Some of the people I met included:

Jerald Tanner who wrote concerning his conversion out of Mormonism: "I have found more and more proof that the church I was raised in is in error...I found that I was a sinner in need of a Saviour. The Mormon Church taught me good morals, but they had not taught me concerning the power of Christ which could change my life...."

Robert C. Witte, organizer of Ex-Mormons for Jesus, in a letter to his Stake president, said: "When I had my personal encounter with Jesus Christ, I was not seeking to question the Mormon Church doctrine, authority or truthfulness. But the Lord led me to the truth about Himself. By means of the written word, and much prayer on my part, He showed me that my Mormon theology was in error."

Melaine Layton, one of the charter members of Ex-Mormons for Jesus, wrote, "My husband and I were born and raised as Mormons. Two years ago we came to know and accept Christ into our hearts as Lord and Saviour. We had been Mormons for 32 years when we were drawn out of the bondage of darkness into God's loving light of truth. I still love the Mormon people very much and respect them very highly for their dedication to what they honestly believe to be true...."

A book such as *Will the "Saints" Go Marching In?* is important to the non-Mormon and Mormon alike: to the non-Mormon who could be influenced by deceitful doctrine that appeals to the flesh but only leads to eternal destruction of the soul; to the Mormon who can know the facts surrounding the origin and evolution of his church, and how it compares with the story he has been taught.

Author Floyd C. McElveen imparts valuable information to the Christian who is seeking answers to the claims of Joseph Smith. McElveen's book is contemporary, complete, and written with a sincere concern that the truth be known. In it, readers will find a storehouse of pertinent information that will assist them in sharing the truth of God's Word with the followers of Joseph Smith.

Jerry Urban
Deerfield, Illinois

Preface

Is it fair, is it Christian to examine Joseph Smith and to question Mormonism?

This is a question I had to pray about and settle before I wrote this book. Insofar as God has given me the light to see from His Word, the following is what I believe He has shown.

Every man has the God-given right to believe as he sees fit. America has recognized that God-given right. We may freely choose to be Christian or pagan, atheist or believer, Buddhist or Moslem, Baptist, Mormon or Catholic. Thank God for this cherished freedom. It is God, not man, who holds us responsible for the consequences of that choice.

The Authority of Love
One of the foremost badges of the true Christian is love.

John 13:35 says, "By this shall all men know that ye are my disciples, if ye have love one to another." Some people believe that this means we should never look critically at another person's religion. "Knocking somebody else's religion isn't love!" Certainly this is true if we have not first looked very critically and carefully at our own religion and compared it with God's standard, the Bible.

Another response we might get from those who question our authority to witness is "Judge not lest ye be judged." Matthew 7:1 says, "Judge not, that ye be not judged," but according to Matthew 7:5 this verse is addressed to *hypocrites*. On the other hand John 7:24 tells *Christians* to "judge righteous judgment," not according to appearance but according to the Word of God.

How tragic today that some of us Christians in the name of love have withheld the truth from those in error, lest we offend or because we did not love enough. Remember, real love warns.

It is true that we should not major on minors. It may be unnecessary to tell our neighbor that he has bad breath, or that a shingle on his roof is loose. However, it is criminal not to wake him up if he is asleep inside his house and his house is on fire. No excuse, and no empty professions of love will ever satisfy God in such cases.

The Authority of Defense

How does all of this apply to the question, "Is it fair, is it Christian, to examine Joseph Smith and question Mormonism?" It is fair because Joseph Smith first attacked all Christians and their churches. Joseph Smith declared in his inspired *Pearl of Great Price,* that all other churches are wrong, all their creeds are an abomination, and all their professors are corrupt.

In one sweep, Joseph Smith condemns all churches, and all their beliefs, and all Christians. He is plainly saying that there was not one true Christian upon the face of the earth at the time he had his first vision, and there hadn't been for hundreds of years.

We have been challenged by Mormon leaders to examine the *Book of Mormon,* which naturally would include its author and its followers. Mormon apostle, Orson Pratt, said:

"This book must be either true or false...If false, it is one of the most cunning, wicked, bold, deep laid impositions ever palmed upon the world, calculated to deceive and ruin millions who will sincerely receive it as the Word of God, and will suppose themselves securely built upon the rock of truth until they are plunged with their families into hopeless despair. The nature of the message in the *Book of Mormon* is such that, if true, no one can possibly be saved and reject it; if false, no one can possibly be saved and receive it. Therefore, every soul in all the world is equally interested in ascertaining its truth or falsity...If, after a rigid examination, it be found an imposition, it should be extensively published to the world as such; the evidences and arguments on which the imposture was detected, should be clearly and logically stated, that those who have been sincerely yet unfortunately deceived, may perceive the nature of the deception and be reclaimed, and that those who continue to publish the delusion, may be exposed and silenced...by evidences adduced from Scripture and reason." [1]

We couldn't agree more! It is Christian to examine Joseph Smith and question Mormonism, because we are commanded to, both for our sake and for the sake of all Mormons.

It is both Christian and sensible to examine Joseph Smith because he claims to be a prophet of God, and we are told, "by their fruits ye shall know them." *The Book of Mormon, Pearl of Great Price, Doctrine and Covenants,* and Mormonism and the whole Mormon movement hinge entirely on this one basic question, "Is Joseph Smith truly a prophet of God?"

We wonder if a teen-age boy today had a vision telling him

that all Mormons were apostate, corrupt, their creeds an abomination to God, if Mormons would embrace his unwitnessed story as quickly as they did that of Joseph Smith? Why not?

With God's help, we will seek to take a fair and honest look at Joseph Smith and a few of his teachings as Scripture and the love of Christ constrain us to. God loves Mormons and non-Mormons. Christ died for each of us. There is no difference before God in that all of us are simply sinners needing a Saviour. In that sense, we are all on common ground. We need to make a firm and clear distinction between Mormonism and Mormons. We pray God will break our hearts and fill us with His love for Mormons, and we think He has. God, and perhaps others, can judge that better than we can. But loving the Mormon people is far different from loving Mormonism, just as God can love the sinner, but not his sin. Please keep that distinction in mind as we consider the claims of Joseph Smith and Mormonism.

Footnote

1. Orson Pratt, *Divine Authority of the Book of Mormon,* introduction, a series of pamphlets published in 1850–51. Quoted by Arthur Budvarson, the *Book of Mormon—True or False?* (Concord, Calif.: Pacific Pub. Co., 1959).

CHAPTER ONE

My Introduction to Mormonism, and to Christ

Man, was I excited! I had just moved from muggy Mississippi to the crisp, cool nights and sparkling days of LaGrande, Oregon, in July. My beautiful wife and my brand new baby boy of less than two months were sharing the adventure only a little less enthusiastically.

I loved my native south, but the heat was getting to me. I had visited Oregon while I was in the Navy, and enjoyed its cool nights, wild game, and beautiful mountains. My uncle had operated a store in Bates, Oregon. An aunt had attended Eastern Oregon College of Education at LaGrande. So after my Navy days I went back to LaGrande, enrolled in the college and played one year of football.

Many of the girls were lovely, but I wanted a girl who could bake cornbread. I found her at the University of Southern Mississippi. Now I was back in fascinating Oregon, preparing for a deer hunt for some urgently needed meat. Not knowing the country too well and not owning a car, I had made friends with a local teen-age boy and hoped to hunt the nearby Blue mountains with him.

"Hey Mike, hurry up!" I groused at him, one scintillatingly beautiful Sunday afternoon. "If you'll quit messing around we can play a little ball and still have time to scout the mountains for deer and find out where the big bucks are before the season opens."

"O.K. I'll hurry and get—" Mike began.

"No you won't!" exploded Mike's older married brother John. As I looked at him in surprise he continued. "We are Mormons, belonging to the Latter-Day Saints church and we do not believe in doing things like that on Sunday."

I was both stunned and chagrined. Back in rural Mississippi, practically everybody was a Baptist unless he'd been meddled with. We had gone to church every Sunday faithfully. I had gone forward at 12, told the evangelist I believed in Jesus, been baptized, joined the church, attended faithfully and didn't drink, smoke or curse. Hunting or fishing on Sunday was only for pagans and backsliders, and you didn't want to be too near someone like that in a lightning storm. I had been a Boy Scout leader, and a Sunday School teacher, yet here I was getting a lecture from a Mormon about God and Sunday. I was ashamed. I was also curious.

John was my local barber, and a very good friend. He was also a wheel in the local LDS church. (I didn't know the terminology then.) We ate in his house and he ate in ours. In fact, I will never forget one "squirrel banquet" we shared. We were poor, and food, especially meat, was scarce. I feel sorry for those poor unsuspecting little pine tree squirrels now, but I didn't then. One thing I will say. The survivors were a lot smarter when I left than they were when I got there.

John was such a kind and gentle man, and a good conversationalist. (That's the kind that lets you talk a lot while they mostly listen.) I was attracted to him and his wife right off, especially when he didn't scalp me when cutting my hair. We had not talked about religion up to now.

I had some serious questions about religion after viewing suicide planes, mutilated and dying buddies in the war; and again while taking courses in various colleges in psychology, evolution, comparative religions, etc. Suddenly, here it was. Here was a man who believed and practiced what he stood for. Why hadn't my church brought me to the convictions he seemed to possess? Yes, I was curious.

"May I come to your house and share with you what Mormons believe?" John asked.

"Certainly," I responded eagerly.

My wife looked somewhat askance at the arrangement, but went along with it. I did not know the difference at the time, but she was a real Christian, with Christ dwelling in her heart. I was only a professing Christian with a head belief. She thought I was a real Christian, as we attended church together, prayed together, tithed, and lived a good life. I had gotten a little bored with church, and she felt something was not quite right, and the pastor of the Conservative Baptist Church in LaGrande, Rev. Guy Zehring, had begun to visit me periodically. I was also bored with him. He repeated things I'd heard all my life. God loves you. Christ died for you. You ought to be faithful in church.

As John began to introduce me to Mormonism, I became intensely interested. Maybe this *was* the answer!

"Wow, John," I cried, after one session, "You mean I can really be married to my wife for all eternity?"

"It's possible," he assured me, "with some conditions that have to be met. You may even be a god on a planet and continue to have children."

This was so appealing to me. Dad died when I was four. I

went to live with my grandfather. He was murdered a few months later. My grandmother got diabetes and, when I was a young teenager, she died a slow, agonizing death. I was almost afraid to fully love anything or anyone. Nothing seemed secure. Nothing was mine to keep and love really, so why break my heart to pieces?

I can still remember the rainy funerals—the cold clods of dirt falling with such dreadful finality on the casket of dad, granddad, grandmother, all so dear to my little heart. The "Old Rugged Cross," valiantly striving to drown out the sobs of loved ones.

Now I had a beautiful young wife. Miracle of miracles, she loved me and I loved her. Was there really a way that I could keep her forever?

Generally happy-go-lucky on the surface, I did some serious thinking in the dark of the night. Someday, her beauty would fade. She would grow old and die soon, so soon, and it would be as if she had never been. Or accident or disease would snatch her from me or me from her. Death was an implacable ogre in ambush, ready to pounce day or night, heeding neither the peal of happy laughter, nor the cry of despair and distress.

As John continued to teach me, I became very confused. "Doesn't the Bible say somewhere that there will be no marrying, neither giving in marriage in heaven, John?"

"Sure," he agreed smoothly, "but that only concerns heaven. We can be married for eternity down here so there won't have to be any marrying or giving in marriage in heaven."

Is that really what that verse means? I wondered. Well, maybe. I sure hope so.

John said that my church had no authority to baptize, make converts, or preach the gospel. The true Church had totally vanished off the earth a century or two after Christ, and God had restored the gospel through a modern-day prophet named Joseph Smith. God and His Son had appeared to the seeking

Smith when he was 14 and begun a series of visions to him concerning God, gold plates and the gospel. Joseph Smith had, by direct revelation from God, translated the inspired *Book of Mormon*. Later inspired books of Mormonism included the *Pearl of Great Price*, and *Doctrine and Covenants*.

John told me gently but firmly quoting Joseph Smith in *Pearl of Great Price* 2:19, in part, "They [the churches] were all wrong... all their creeds were an abomination in his sight; that those professors were corrupt."

This bothered me considerably. The Mormon creed said many of the same things other church creeds said. How could one be totally wrong and abominable and the other O.K.? I knew that many Christians down through the centuries, hundreds of years after the Mormons claimed the true Church and the true gospel had totally vanished in apostasy from the earth, had sealed their love and their testimony for Christ in their blood. Were they all corrupt as Joseph Smith claimed?

John taught me that the Mormon church was the one true Church on the face of the whole earth. All others were false. The only way to the highest heaven or degree of glory was to leave my church and be baptized into the Mormon church. There were three heavens, or three degrees of glory. Only Mormons could go to the highest heaven. Christ's death on the cross gave all men general salvation from hell, except some very few obstinate Sons of Perdition. Personal salvation depended on one's good works. Baptism for the dead was for those who had not had the opportunity to be saved here. They could be saved after death.

I became more and more interested, but also more and more confused. I called Pastor Guy Zehring and tried to compare his answers with John's.

It really seemed to me that John was getting the best of the discussion. I prayed desperately for light. John asked me to take the *Book of Mormon,* lay my hand on it, and pray that if it were truly the Word of God and Mormonism was true to

17

convince me of it by God's Holy Spirit. I did just that. I also prayed the same way about the Bible.

Then, in a puckish spirit, I thought the answer might be in getting John and Guy together and letting them debate the issue. Guy advised me against it, saying it probably wouldn't solve anything for me. I wondered if maybe he was afraid.

By this time I knew that I had to make a decision: become a Mormon or go back to the Christianity I knew which had never met my deepest longings; look deeper into Christianity; forget the whole mess. Each one of these options looked appealing at times.

Finally, I hovered just on the brink of becoming a Mormon. The Mormons I knew were so nice. Their youth program was attractive in the extreme. Some of their churches even had gyms! Their church-sponsored dances looked very inviting. They went out after people to share their faith with them. They were very clean and hard workers. I admired their ruggedness, and reveled in their courageous history of Western migration against impossible odds. Their strong convictions attracted me. They seemed to have such a sense of authority, and so much unity.

One last time, I went to my bedroom, fell on my knees and called out in an agony of need, "God, *please* show me the true way. I don't care which way it is, just so it's from you and the true way. Oh God, I want to be saved so badly. I thought I was when I said I accepted Christ and joined the Baptist church years ago, Lord, but now I am upset. If Mormonism is right I'll gladly accept it and follow it forever. If what I have been taught is right why hasn't it fully met my needs? Oh God, help me. Give me your light. Show me the truth about the Bible and the *Book of Mormon,* about Mormonism and Christianity, and most of all about yourself and how I can be saved and sure of heaven."

Shortly after this honest, searching prayer, I was feverishly getting ready for deer season, which opened the next day. My wife looked outside and said, "Honey, Pastor Guy Zehring just drove up."

"Oh, no," I groaned. I had work to do to prepare to leave for the hunting trip and the pastor had already talked to me five or six times saying practically the same things every time. It seemed so foolish, so unreal and empty. I had a hard time being polite. Only years later did I learn that the Bible says that "The preaching of the cross is to them that perish foolishness" (1 Cor. 1:18).

This time was different. Guy looked me in the eye and said, "Mac, you claim to be a Christian. Do you really know for sure that if you were to die this minute, you'd go to heaven to be with Jesus Christ?"

I bristled. "Nobody can know that for sure," I declared. "I believe that I would go to heaven. I believe in Jesus Christ. I have been baptized, I am religious and I lead a good life. But you said *know*."

Guy's rapier eyes pierced into my very soul. "Mac, if you died tonight, you'd go straight to hell."

"I have done everything you preachers said to do," I answered, "everything I know that the Bible says to do. Does the Bible say that you can know that you are saved?"

"It certainly does," he replied, turning to 1 John 5:13. "These things have I written unto you that believe on the name of the Son of God; that ye may know that ye have eternal life, and that ye may believe on the name of the Son of God."

I was aware of both astonishment and an intense hunger beginning to build inside of me. I had been studying chapters and books of the *Book of Mormon,* and had read the Bible for many years, but nothing had ever spoken to my heart and to my need like this. In spite of occasional doubts, I was really impressed by the Bible. I knew that many of the prophecies of the Bible concerning Jesus Christ, cities, nations and events had come true in every detail. Just the year before, 1948, after 2500 years, the Jews had reestablished the nation of Israel, and this against incredible odds, just as the Bible explicitly predicted. They had retained their identity while bigger, stronger nations had become dusty archeological statistics hundreds of years gone by.

"How did I miss it, Guy," I asked, almost beseechingly. "Why don't I know?"

"You believed all the facts about Jesus," Guy retorted, "His death, burial, resurrection. But yours is a head belief, not a heart belief. Thousands are just like you—religious but lost. You have a historical belief like saying you believe that George Washington crossed the Delaware. But have you ever come to Jesus Christ as a lost sinner and asked Him to save you, and know that He did it?"

"I have asked Him to save me, but I never really had faith that He did it."

"Don't you see," countered Guy, "salvation is by faith, by trust, by believing. Ephesians 2:8,9 declares: 'For by grace are ye saved through faith; and that not of yourselves: it is the gift of God: not of works, lest any man should boast.' "

"Now," he continued, "John 1:12 tells us that we are not by nature children of God. That's our big problem. We have to receive Jesus Christ by personal invitation into our hearts and lives in order to become children of God. We are thus born again into the family of God and instantly receive His free gift of everlasting life. 'But as many as received him, to them gave he power to become the sons of God, even to them that believe on his name.' Then and only then are we ready for heaven."

He added, "Jesus loves us so much He died in bloody torture for us. He promised to save us if we would believingly call on Him. When you called, and then wondered or hoped maybe He had done what He died to do and promised to do, you were in essence doubting Him and making Him a liar. Therefore He could not save you, even if you had wept and cried and pleaded to be saved every night for a hundred years, because He only saves by faith. Romans 10:9 tells us that only a heart belief, committal to Christ as the resurrected Lord (God and master) and Saviour can save us."

"Romans 10:13 makes it so clear and simple, a child can understand it, 'For whosoever shall call upon the name of the Lord shall be saved.'

"Mac," Guy said quietly but feelingly, "God loves you. Jesus shed His blood for you. If you ask Him, believing with all your heart, to save you, He will have to save you. Otherwise He would be a liar, because He promised. Will you call upon Him to save you right now?"

Oh, the battle that raged in my heart! Could it really be that simple? Was it for real? Suppose there was a burning hell, after all, and there was even the slightest chance that I might go there for eternity. Was Jesus really the eternal God, as Guy said the Bible declared Him to be? Did He rise bodily and appear to hundreds who touched Him, ate with Him and later died for Him?

Suddenly I knew. If I couldn't trust the simple clear promise of Jesus who died for me, where else was there to go? The desperate longing in me cried out for Jesus, for certainty, and I fell on my knees and poured out my heart to Him and asked Him to come into my heart and forgive me all my sins. I asked Him to make me a child of God forever, and give me everlasting life. I asked Him for a know-so salvation, and took Him as my very own personal Lord and Saviour.

I got to my feet and wiped away a tear. Guy pointed his stubby finger at me and asked, "Did Jesus save you or did He lie? He had to do one or the other."

Inside of me I knew something tremendous had happened. A burden I didn't even know I was carrying was gone; joy and peace unspeakable filled my heart. But after years of psychology, I was not about to depend just on experience, emotions or feelings. So I just said to Guy, "Well, He couldn't lie, so He must have saved me."

Guy turned to John 3:36. "He that believeth on the Son hath

everlasting life." I looked very carefully at that verse, savoring every word. Then I knew, not just felt. *Knew!* Jesus had saved me! I now had, right now, everlasting life. His Word said so and He cannot lie. His Holy Spirit witnessed with my spirit that I was His child, sure of heaven with Him in accord with His written Word. Guy and I knelt again and I thanked God very simply for having saved my soul and giving me everlasting life.

I couldn't wait to tell John! I knew instantly when I was truly saved that Mormonism was not the way. It was as if God turned a great searchlight on the whole system and revealed His answer to me. But I dearly loved John, and wanted to share my joy and utter certainty with him. I gathered up all the considerable Mormon material he had given me and hurried over to his house.

"John, John," I cried. "I've found Jesus. I've just been saved and I know I am going to heaven!"

"You've been hypnotized!" he roared, turning red in the face.

"Don't you know for sure that you have been saved, John?" I asked.

"No and you don't either," he asserted, growing more agitated by the moment.

I was shocked. Could this be my gentle, loving John. Why wasn't he rejoicing at my joy in finding Christ?

"John," I inquired seriously, "do you mean to tell me that all this time you've been talking to me about being in the one true Church, about having prophets and priests, about authority, that you don't even know for sure where you are going when you die?

"Suppose I was lost in the woods with a number of other people. Suppose we were desperate with just time to get out if we chose the right trail right away, before we starved or froze to death. Suppose we bumped into you, and you declared you had an infallible map, and that you were a licensed guide for those woods and insisted that we all follow you, all other trails were wrong. Then suppose I asked you if you knew for sure that you were not lost, that you knew just where you were. And you admitted you did not, and were not even sure where you were going. John, I love you, but I know I am saved, and I cannot go your way any longer."

With that I gave John back his material on Mormonism. John and I continued to be friends. Often he visited me with Mormon leaders to try to win me back. I was touched with his obvious concern, his caring. But I knew I would never again be among those the Bible says are "ever learning but never coming to a knowledge of the truth" (see 2 Tim. 3:7).

Once you've truly met Jesus the search is over. I had read my Bible and attended church all my life, but I had missed it. I'd prayed daily, and on long, moonlit walks had often felt the warm presence of Jesus. I believed that I loved Him, but this was different, richer, sweeter by far.

Before salvation was like loving a girl and having a certain amount of communion with her before marriage, but she doesn't belong to you nor do you belong to her. Then, in the simple act of marriage, you say "I do" and she does too. There is no magic in the words, but, if it is true love, your lives are changed forever. She belongs to you and you belong to her. What you thought was love before is no comparison to what you have now. With real salvation, when you get married to Jesus in an act the Bible calls conversion, you *know* the difference. Before, I was religious but lost. Now I am saved.

John has never understood though I've prayed for him and wept for him with a real ache in my heart.

Now years later, after spending thousands of hours in Bible study and reading dozens of Mormon books and booklets—both pro and con—I want to share with other hungry hearts, in Christ's love and as God enables me, what He has shown me.

CHAPTER TWO

Joseph Smith and the First Vision

Many who read this book may well ask, "Where did the Mormons get such different ideas about God and about Christ? What is the source of their doctrine? Where did their church really originate? What is the foundation on which their beliefs rest?"

Very briefly, the Mormons teach that the true gospel disappeared off the earth shortly after the time of the apostolic church. They believe that *all* churches then became false, and that they had no authority from God. All the professing Christians for hundreds of years were corrupt, false, apostate. Then God *restored* the true gospel with its pristine authority through a young man named Joseph Smith. An angel appeared in a vision to young Joseph and subsequently led him to some golden plates hidden near Palmyra, New York. From these plates, God enabled Joseph Smith to produce the *Book of Mormon,* the first and foundational inspired book on which Mormonism is based.

Since Joseph Smith declared all other churches without exception to be false and all their members to be corrupt, it only seems fair to answer him. If Joseph Smith was a true prophet of God, then the First Vision should be clear and unassailable, as God is not the author of confusion. But let us hear from Mormon sources as to the importance of this First Vision.

David O. McKay, Mormon apostle and leader, stated: "The appearing of the Father and the Son to Joseph Smith is the foundation of this Church."[1]

First Vision of 1820

The Mormon apostle John A. Widtsoe said: "The First Vision of 1820 is of first importance in the history of Joseph Smith. Upon its reality rest the truth and value of his subsequent work."[2]

Obviously, the integrity of Joseph Smith and the truth of Mormonism are at stake. If the First Vision is the foundation on which Mormonism rests, let us prayerfully and carefully examine that foundation.

The Mormon church claims that Joseph Smith had a vision in 1820, when he was a 14-year-old boy. This vision occurred on the "morning of a beautiful, clear day, early in the spring of eighteen hundred and twenty." Joseph Smith had gone to the woods to pray about which of "all the sects was right." While in prayer he saw two personages standing above him in the air. One of the personages pointed to the other and said, "This is My Beloved Son. Hear Him!" Then one of the personages, whom Joseph Smith identifies as the Father and the Son, told him that all churches were wrong.

26

Strangely enough, there is no mention of this vision in the early Mormon church records and the *Improvement Era,* admits: "Joseph Smith's 'official' account of his first vision and the visits of the angel Moroni was...first published in the *Times and Seasons* in 1842."[3] This is 22 years after the event is supposed to have occurred. Yet the first vision is supposed to be the *foundation* of the Mormon church, which began in 1830! The *Book of Mormon* was published in 1830 also. Why didn't Joseph Smith give an official account of the vision before 1842?

For years, Mormons emphatically declared, "Joseph Smith lived a little more than 24 years after this first vision. During this time he told but one story!"[4] This, of course, is not true. Jerald and Sandra Tanner, in their pamphlet, *The First Vision Examined,* have shown that two versions other than his "official" version, existed in the Mormon church, but were not published until exposure by Paul Cheesman, a student at Brigham Young University, in 1965.

Another account of the First Vision came to light through James B. Allen, associate professor of History at BYU, in 1966, after Mormon denials for years that there were any other versions! These versions contain important discrepancies from the official version. For a detailed and scholarly explanation, get the Tanners' pamphlet, *The First Vision Examined.*

Even Brigham Young, who had 363 of his sermons recorded in the *Journal of Discourses,* as an "inspired" apostle succeeding Joseph Smith, failed to mention the First Vision. Mormon librarian Lauritz G. Petersen in a letter dated August 31, 1959, wrote: "I have checked through the *Journal of Discourses* which records many of the sermons of Brigham Young. There is no mention there of anything by Brigham Young on the first vision of Joseph Smith."[5]

Oddly enough Oliver Cowdery, the first Mormon historian (according to *Doctrines of Salvation,* vol. 2, p. 201), did not even refer to the First Vision. Cowdery was one of the three main witnesses to the *Book of Mormon*. Yet Earl E. Olsen, Mormon librarian, L.D.S. Church, wrote in a letter dated March 24, 1958, "In the records which we have on file of the writings of Oliver Cowdery, and John Whitmer, such as they are, we do not find a reference to the First Vision."[6]

First Vision of 1823

It has come to light nevertheless, that Oliver Cowdery, assisted for accuracy by Joseph Smith himself, did publish an account of the First Vision in the Mormon *Messenger and Advocate,* in September, 1834, and in February, 1835, differing in important respects from the later "official" 1842 version. Actually, the first reports in the Mormon Church of Joseph Smith's First Vision claimed that he was *17* years old, not *14*.

(Good Mormon friends, in honest puzzlement over the clear contradictions and confusion we are about to present, have told us we had Joseph Smith's First Vision confused with another vision or visions that he had. We sympathize with their heartbreak over what the following facts will reveal. However, we have read many of Joseph Smith's visions and we are well aware of them, as numbers of other students of Mormonism are. The vision we are discussing was plainly declared, by Joseph Smith himself and other Mormon authorities, to be the First Vision. We must face reality, gently, but firmly.)

Orville Spencer, a leading Mormon in the early church, wrote a letter from Nauvoo, Illinois, in 1842, stating: "Joseph Smith, when the great designs of heaven were first made known to him, was not far from the age of seventeen."[7]

Now this is in accord with the account of Smith's age, *17 years old in 1823,* when first reports of a vision were given, as proven from the *Messenger and Advocate,* volume 1, pages 78, 79, referring to a revival that is supposed to have taken place in and around Palmyra, New York, at about the time of Joseph Smith's vision. "While this excitement continued, he continued to call upon the Lord in secret for a full manifestation of

divine approbation and for, to him, the all important information, *if a supreme being did exist,* to have an assurance that he
was accepted of Him.... On the evening of the 21st of September, 1823, previous to retiring to rest, our brother's mind
was unusually wrought upon the subject which had so long
agitated his mind—his heart was drawn out in fervent prayer
... while continuing in prayer for a manifestation in some way
that his sins were forgiven; endeavoring to exercise faith in the
Scriptures, on a sudden a light like that of day, only of a purer
and far more glorious appearance and brightness, burst into the
room... and in a moment a personage stood before him... he
heard him declare himself to be a messenger sent by the
commandment of the Lord, to deliver a special message, and to
witness to him that his sins were forgiven."[8]

Notice please, this is a Mormon source, and an official
Mormon account admitting that *Joseph Smith at 17, in 1823,*
did not even know whether or not there was a Supreme Being,
even though later Mormons claim he had a vision of the *Father*
and the *Son* at *age 14, in 1820!* In fact, Mormon leader and
apostle David O. McKay declared that this First Vision that
Joseph Smith claimed he had at age 14, was the *foundation* of
the Mormon church! Why then, did Joseph Smith not even
know if a Supreme Being existed when he was 17 years old
in 1823?

First Vision and Angels

Furthermore, in the *Deseret News,* May 29, 1852, Joseph
Smith was quoted as having said, "I received the first visitation
of angels, which was when I was about fourteen years old."
This points out another discrepancy from many Mormon
sources. The early accounts of the vision list an *angel* appearing to Joseph Smith, not the Father and the Son.

Apostle Orson Pratt stated: "By and by an obscure individual, a young man, rose up, and, in the midst of all Christendom, proclaimed the startling news that God had sent an angel

to him;...This occurred before this young man was fifteen years of age."[9] This is obviously referring to Smith's First Vision.

John Taylor, the third president of the Mormon church, stated; "How did this state of things called Mormonism *originate*? We read that an *angel* came down and revealed himself to Joseph Smith and manifested unto him in vision the true position of the world in a religious point of view."[10]

In spite of this irrefutable evidence from Mormon apostles themselves, the story of the First Vision *grew* and was *changed* until today's version: that Joseph Smith saw the Father and the Son. According to the current version in 1820, when he was 14 years old, Joseph Smith saw a pillar of light. "It no sooner appeared than I found myself delivered from the enemy which held me bound. When the light rested upon me I saw two Personages, whose brightness and glory defy all description, standing above me in the air. One of them spake unto me, calling me by name and said, pointing to the other, *This is my Beloved Son. Hear Him!*"[11]

Neither Joseph Smith, nor inspired Mormon apostles quoting him, stuck to the original story about *the year, Joseph's age, or the content of the vision.*

First Vision and the Priesthood

Joseph Smith himself gave positive evidence that he did *not* see the Father and the Son in 1820. In 1832 Joseph Smith claimed to have a revelation from God which stated that a man could *not* see God without the priesthood. By Joseph Smith's own admission, he was not a priest in 1820, nor did he even claim to be granted this office until sometime in the early 1830s![12]

Joseph Smith's 1832 revelation concerning the priesthood is recorded in section 84 of *Doctrine and Covenants,* verses 21,22, "And without the ordinances thereof, and the Authority of the Priesthood, the power of godliness is not manifest unto men in the flesh, for without this no man can see the face of God, even the Father, and live."

Mormon apostle Parley P. Pratt declared, "The truth is this: that without the Priesthood of Melchisedek, 'no man can see God and live!' "[13] Joseph Smith was *not* a priest in *1820*. If his revelation that no man could see God without the priesthood was true, then Joseph Smith had never seen God, and his claim in 1842 of having seen God in 1820 was not true. If his 1820 claim was true, then his revelation from God in 1832 that no man could see God without the priesthood was false. Either way, this would label Joseph Smith as one who was not a prophet of God.

Moroni or Nephi

Another problem worth mentioning in this connection is that the angel who is supposed to have appeared to Joseph Smith is almost always named Moroni, both by Joseph Smith and other Mormon writers. Nonetheless, in the 1851 first edition of the *Pearl of Great Price,* page 41, the angel's name was Nephi, not Moroni. Further proof of this may be found in *Times and Seasons,* volume 3, pages 749 and 753, *and* in the writings of the mother of Joseph Smith, Lucy Mack Smith, in her *Biographical Sketches,* 1853.

In Summary

Some observations about Joseph Smith and the First Vision seem in order. Former president and inspired Mormon apostle David O. McKay declared that the First Vision is the foundation of the Mormon church. On this all the authority that Mormons claim they have ultimately rests.

We ask why so many Mormon leaders, apostles, presidents, and writers are so *confused* about what Joseph Smith saw or didn't see? Why did Joseph Smith himself give several utterly irreconcilable accounts of the First Vision? Why did Joseph Smith's and the Mormon's official version not come out until

1842 if this vision is so important to Mormonism? The church began in 1830, and the *Book of Mormon* was published in 1830, yet the 1820 vision upon which the church is *founded,* is not officially given until 1842!

Why do we have contradictory "revelations" from God to His inspired apostle? God never contradicts Himself. When any word, or revelation, is contradictory, it cannot be from God. Did Joseph Smith really have a vision? If so, when? At what age? What did he really see? Was it a good angel or an evil angel, if he had a vision? Was it from God or from one of Satan's spirits appearing as an angel of light? "And no marvel; for Satan himself is transformed into an angel of light. Therefore it is no great thing if his ministers also be transformed as the ministers of righteousness" (2 Cor. 11:14,15).

Think again about the contradictions as to the time of the vision, the age of Joseph Smith, and the content of the vision. Think about Joseph getting a revelation in 1832 revealing that only those ordained to the priesthood could see God and live, yet he was supposed to have seen God in 1820, many years before he was made a priest by his own testimony. First Corinthians 14:33: "For God is not the author of confusion, but of peace, as in all churches of the saints."

It can be little comfort to know that many cults began with a vision or claims of a vision because they would not believe the Word of God, or because they believed the Word of God was not enough. God therefore sent them "strong delusion" that they should believe a lie (see 2 Thess. 2:10-12).

Finally, Mormons need to seriously consider Galatians 1:8. "But though we, or an angel from heaven, preach any other gospel unto you than that which we have preached unto you, let him be accursed."

If this First Vision is the foundation, let's see what Joseph Smith built on it.

1. David O. McKay, *Gospel Ideals* (Salt Lake City: The Church of Jesus Christ of Latter-day Saints, 1953), p. 85.

2. John A. Widtsoe, *Joseph Smith—Seeker After Truth* (Salt Lake City: Deseret Book Co., 1951), p. 19.

3. *Improvement Era,* July 1961, p. 490. (A monthly periodical published by The Church of Jesus Christ of Latter-day Saints.)

4. *Joseph Smith, the Prophet,* 1944, p. 30. Quoted in Jerald and Sandra Tanner, *The First Vision Examined* (Salt Lake City: Modern Microfilm Co., 1969), p. 2.

5. Jerald Tanner, *Mormonism*: A Study of Mormon History and Doctrine (Clearfield, Utah: Utah Evangel Press, 1962), p. 79.

6. Tanner, *Mormonism,* p. 8.

7. *Millenial Star,* vol. 4, p. 37.

8. *Messenger and Advocate,* vol. 1, pp. 78, 79. Quoted in Tanner, *The First Vision Examined* (Salt Lake City: Modern Microfilm Co., 1969), p. 15.

9. *Journal of Discourses* (Liverpool, England: F. D. and S. W. Richards, Pub; 1854. Reprinted edition, Salt Lake City, 1966), vol. 13, pp. 65, 66. The *Journal of Discourses* is a collection of sermons by Brigham Young, Orson Pratt, Heber Kimball and others from 1854 to 1886.

10. *Journal of Discourses,* vol. 10, p. 127.

11. Joseph Smith, *Pearl of Great Price* (Salt Lake City: The Church of Jesus Christ of Latter-day Saints, 1958), p. 48, #17.

12. Bruce R. McConkie, ed., *Doctrines of Salvation* (Salt Lake City: Bookcraft, Inc., 1954), vol. 1, p. 4.

13. Parley P. Pratt, *Writings of Parley P. Pratt,* p. 306. Quoted by Jerald and Sandra Tanner, *Mormonism, Shadow or Reality* (Salt Lake City: Modern Microfilm Co., 1972) p. 144.

CHAPTER THREE

Joseph Smith— Prophet of God?

Was Joseph Smith a prophet of God? I am so thankful that God did not leave such important decisions up to the opinions or whims of men. He gave an absolutely infallible test so that the simplest Christian could determine whether or not a professed prophet was true or false. It is so clear that even those who are not Christians can apply it and not be led astray in their search for truth.

Here is God's test for a prophet: "But the prophet, which shall presume to speak a word in my name, which I have not commanded him to speak, or that shall speak in the name of other gods, even that prophet shall die. And if thou say in thine heart, How shall we know the word which the Lord hath not spoken? When a prophet speaketh in the name of the Lord, if the thing follow not, nor come to pass, that is the thing which the Lord hath not spoken, but the prophet hath spoken it presumptuously: thou shalt not be afraid of him" (Deut. 18:20-22).

From this as well as numerous other Bible passages we know that God spoke through His true prophets, as they prophesied, word for word. Since God cannot lie or be mistaken, His *true* prophets were *always* accurate in fulfillment. Any prophet not meeting this test of fulfilled prophecy was a false prophet. (See Deut. 13:1-5; Isa. 9:13-16; Jer. 14:13-16; Ezek. 13:1-9.)

One false prophecy would forever disqualify a man as a prophet of God. According to the Scriptures a false prophet would have been killed for presuming to speak that which God had not spoken, under Old Testament law.

Following are a few of Joseph Smith's prophecies that did not meet God's simple test of accuracy:

1. Concerning the New Jerusalem and its Temple (Rev. 21:22). According to this prophecy in *Doctrine and Covenants* 84:1-5, given September 1832, the city and temple are to be built in Missouri in *this* (the current) generation. The apostles of the Mormon church knew about this prophecy and declared in the *Journal of Discourses* (vol. 9, p. 71; vol. 10, p. 344; vol. 13, p. 362), their certainty that this prophecy would come to pass within the generation encompassing the 1832 prophecy by Smith. In fact, on May 5, 1870, apostle Orson Pratt staunchly declared: "The Latter-day Saints just as much expect to receive a fulfillment of that promise during the generation that was in existence in 1832 as they expect that the sun will rise and set tomorrow. Why? Because God cannot lie. He will fulfill all His promises."[1]

The city was *not* built; the temple was *not* built in *this* generation. The prophecy was false.

2. Zion, Missouri cannot fall or be moved, *Doctrine and Covenants,* Section 97. Joseph Smith was in Kirtland, Ohio at the time he made this prediction and was unaware that Zion

was moved—two weeks prior to the so-called revelation.

3. Nauvoo House is to belong to the Smith family forever, *Doctrine and Covenants* 124:56-60. Joseph Smith was killed in 1844. The Mormons were driven from Nauvoo and the house no longer belonged to the Smith family. This prophecy was false. Joseph Smith was a false prophet.

4. Joseph Smith's enemies will be confounded when they seek to destroy him, 2 Nephi 3:14, *The Book of Mormon.* Smith was shot in jail in Carthage, Illinois June 27, 1844.

5. Jesus Christ was to be born at Jerusalem, Alma 7:10, *The Book of Mormon.* God's Word says that Jesus would be born in Bethlehem (Mic. 5:2), which prophecy was fulfilled (Matt. 2:1).

6. The coming of the Lord, *History of the Church,* volume 2, page 182. In 1835 prophet-president Joseph Smith predicted "the coming of the Lord, which was nigh...even fifty-six years should wind up the scene."[2]

7. Concerning "moon inhabitants," *Journal of Oliver B. Huntington,* volume 2, page 166. This devout and dedicated Mormon associate of Joseph Smith quoted Joseph Smith describing his revelation concerning the moon and its inhabitants: "The inhabitants of the moon are more of a uniform size than the inhabitants of the earth, being about six feet in height. They dress very much like the Quaker style and are quite general in style, or the fashion of dress. They live to be very old; coming generally near a thousand years."[3]

Joseph Smith undoubtedly never dreamed that men from the earth would one day walk on the moon. He probably felt quite safe in giving this "revelation."

God's test for a prophet is very simple. God's test for a prophet is very clear. Joseph Smith cannot pass the test. His prophecies failed. Joseph Smith was a false prophet.

Mormon friends that I have confronted with this evidence have had various reactions as might be expected. Some have been shaken. They have admitted that Joseph Smith was a false prophet and have turned with all their heart to Jesus Christ alone, much to their joy and mine.

One lovely Mormon lady had labored indefatigably in the Mormon church and had become quite prominent in the women's work in a nearby state. She read this material, talked to me personally and was wonderfully delivered from Mormonism to Christ. She dearly loves the Mormon people and has a tremendous burden for them. Later, I had the inexpressible joy of leading her Mormon husband to Christ. How he wept for joy when Jesus took his sins away and gave him the free gift of everlasting life! Such sure and lasting peace he never found in Mormonism.

Other Mormons, in defense of the *Book of Mormon* and the Mormon church, and in fear of the awesome implications to themselves and their families, refuse to admit the obvious—Joseph Smith was a false prophet. They try desperately or valiantly, depending on your viewpoint, to rescue him from his inextricable dilemma.

"You've taken what he said out of context!" some have declared.

"Maybe he meant something else," was one forlorn rejoinder.

"People in the Bible had faults," several remarked, which has nothing whatever to do with God's test for a prophet.

"I just don't believe Joseph Smith was a false prophet!"

"It's just a bunch of lies!" one dear Mormon soul cried, ignoring the fact that the quotations are almost exclusively from Mormon books, sources, and apostles, and are well documented so that she can check for herself and draw her own conclusions.

Surely all true Christian hearts go out in compassion to Mormons, if there is an ounce of the love of Christ in us. To see and feel the anguish of those who begin to recognize that they have been misled is not pleasant. However, the anguish of a lost eternity without Christ is infinitely more horrible. Real love cannot evade our responsibility. We may feel very much like a doctor who must steel himself to tell a dear friend he has cancer.

The test has been given. Joseph Smith was not a prophet of God. He was a false prophet.

Footnotes

1. Pratt, *Journal of Discourses,* vol. 9, p. 71.
2. Joseph Smith, *History of the Church* (Salt Lake City: The Church of Jesus Christ of Latter-day Saints, 1902–1912), vol. 2, p. 182.
3. Huntington Library, San Marino, California, from the *Journal of Oliver B. Huntington,* vol. 2, p. 166.

CHAPTER FOUR

The Book of Mormon— Joseph Smith's or God's?

God is just as able to preserve His Word, which He promised to do, as He was able to give it in the first place. He has inculcated a fervent fidelity to His Word in the hearts of many godly scholars and translators. Through the centuries, many of His true people have given their lives to preserve the purity of His Word.

Accuracy and Harmony of the Bible

Close to 5,000 manuscripts, and bits and pieces of manuscripts, of the Word of God have been found virtually all over Europe and Asia. So, we do not have to depend on just one translation from one manuscript. The harmony and accuracy of these manuscripts are amazing.

The writings of the church fathers, some of them contemporary with the apostle John, contain the text of practically the entire New Testament. These writings match accurately with the New Testament manuscripts we use. The Dead Sea

Scrolls also harmonize with our later versions. This is further corroboration that we have the Word of God as it was originally given.

The accuracy of the Scriptures is attested to by many erudite biblical scholars. One of these is the former Princetonian scholar and genius Robert Dick Wilson. A devout Christian and a linguist who was conversant with 26 languages, Robert Dick Wilson claimed that he doubted that even one word in a thousand had been changed or carried any different meaning from the original God gave.

Robert Dick Wilson spent a lifetime in careful study of God's Word in the original languages. He was a professor of Semitic Philology at Princeton and indubitably one of the world's great scholars. In reference to the Bible, Robert Dick Wilson summed up his convictions in his book, *A Scientific Investigation of the Old Testament*: "In conclusion, let me reiterate my conviction that no one knows enough to show that the true text of the Old Testament in its true interpretation is not true."[1]

Robert Dick Wilson is only one of many dedicated biblical scholars who has attested to the accuracy of the Bible as we now have it. These people have proven by research what Jesus declared: "Heaven and earth shall pass away, but my words shall not pass away" (Matt. 24:35). And the infallible Son of God is not mistaken, nor does He lie.

We often read of Socrates, and his story is widely accepted without question. However, the proof that Socrates ever lived comes from *one* manuscript by *one* person, Plato! The only other account of this Greek philosopher is in the manuscript of a comical play by a Greek writer named Aristophanes. Yet no one doubts the existence of Socrates.

Much of history that we commonly accept as true, comes to us from very early sources. The story of Julius Caesar and the Gallic wars is recorded in several manuscripts but the oldest is dated 900 years after Caesar's day. Yet we accept, as incontrovertible fact, the verification of this history.

On the other hand we have thousands of manuscripts and portions of manuscripts, from widely differing places concerning Jesus Christ and His Word. This means that no scribe, even if God had allowed it, could have changed something in the translation without its being caught by another biblical scholar. For these manuscripts have been compared assiduously again and again by both the enemies and friends of Jesus Christ.

The Mormon's Acceptance of the Bible

In spite of the overwhelming evidence as to the accuracy and harmony of the Bible, the Mormons profess to believe the Bible, "as far as it is translated correctly."[2] However they do not add any such qualification to their acceptance of the *Book of Mormon* which they declare to be the very Word of God.

To question the Bible is to question the authority and truthfulness of the Lord Jesus Christ. To show how far some Mormons have used this loophole in their "Articles of Faith" to deny the Bible as the infallible Word of God, read what LDS apostle Orson Pratt says in his comments about the Bible: "Who knows that even *one verse* of the Bible has escaped pollution, so as to convey the same sense now that it did in the original?"[3]

We hope we may be pardoned for pointing out that this logic seems just a little suspect. Pratt was writing to prove that the *Book of Mormon* is the inspired Word of God, without error. Since hundreds of verses of the "polluted" Bible were copied verbatim from the much maligned *King James Version* into the *Book of Mormon,* this hardly seems to help his argument! You do not introduce water from a polluted stream into a pure, clear stream and continue to call the one polluted and the other pure!

Joseph Smith copied verses and chapters from all over the Bible. Second Nephi, chapters 12 through 24 in the *Book of Mormon,* is copied mostly word for word from the *King James Version* of Isaiah, chapters 2 through 14.

Revelation for the *Book of Mormon*

In the *Pearl of Great Price,* pages 50–54, Joseph Smith gives an account of a vision he had in 1823. The "messenger sent from the presence of God," Moroni, told him that God had work for him to do. He was to find some gold plates on which was written a book that Joseph Smith was to translate. The messenger told him where the plates were hidden and gave him instructions concerning them.

Also preserved, with the gold plates, were the Urim and Thummin mentioned in the Old Testament (see Exod. 28:30; Num. 27:21; Ezra 2:63). According to Joseph Smith, the Urim and Thummin was a kind of divine spectacles (two stones in silver bowls) God kept for thousands of years and put in a box with the gold plates to help him interpret and translate the language in which the book was written. This language was reformed Egyptian. According to *Doctrine and Covenants,* Joseph Smith declared that God gave him the power to translate the reformed Egyptian hieroglyphics into English and produce the *Book of Mormon.*

Joseph Smith would put on the Urim and Thummin and be able to translate the message on the gold tablets. After Smith translated the first 116 pages of the *Book of Mormon,* which got lost or stolen, an "angel" apparently took these spectacles away. Then Joseph used the "seer stone" or treasure-hunting stone, which was common property in that day of many fortune tellers and treasure seekers, to translate the reformed Egyptian hieroglyphics. This stone is also called the Urim and Thummin by Mormon writers. I wonder why God bothered to provide the spectacles, after preserving them for so many centuries for Joseph Smith to use, when they were so little used and so easily replaced by something else.

According to the three witnesses of the *Book of Mormon,* David Whitmer, Oliver Cowdery and Martin Harris, Smith would put the stone into a hat, and then put his face into the hat as he started to translate from the gold plates. The gold plates were seldom, if ever, present. They seem as superfluous as the Urim and Thummin spectacles. Again, I wonder why Joseph Smith even bothered to dig them up.

David Whitmer, in *Address to All Believers in Christ,* says that as Joseph Smith put his face into his hat with the seer stone, "something resembling parchment would appear."[4] The hieroglyphics would appear, one character at a time, with the English interpretation underneath. Joseph Smith would read it and Oliver Cowdery, or whoever was the amanuensis or secretary at that time would write it. If correctly written, the character or sentence would disappear. If not, it would remain until corrected. This means that every letter, every character, was exactly what God said, letter-by-letter and word-for-word. There could be no mistake because the character or word would not go away until 100 percent accuracy was achieved.

The written word was perfect. And when this 1830 publication of the *Book of Mormon* was printed, Joseph Smith pronounced that book perfect or "correct" also. He should know if he was a true prophet of God.

Some Problems with the *Book of Mormon*

Joseph Smith said this reformed Egyptian was a language known to no man, but was the language that Mormon (the father of Moroni) wrote on the gold plates somewhere around A.D. 384 to 421, just before he died. *It is a problem to many that this language was reproduced in the* Book of Mormon *in the same words of the 1611 King James Bible in hundreds and thousands of instances.*

It doesn't seem likely that reformed Egyptian, a language which was known to no man and which perished from the earth over 1,000 years before 1611, the year the King James Bible was published, would contain thousands of the same words and phrases, in the exact order in which they are found in the King James Version of the Bible. *Even the italicized words in the* King James Version *appear in the* Book of Mormon.

Joseph Smith did not italicize them but included them into the *Book of Mormon* text as if they were the words of God.

The scholars who translated the King James Version italicized certain words to warn the reader that they were not in the original Hebrew or Greek text but were added for smoother reading or explanation. A few of the many examples of italicized words which are in the *King James Version* and the *Book of Mormon* can be seen by comparing Isaiah 53:2,3,4 with Mosiah 14:2,3,5.

Another problem we find with the Book of Mormon *is in the poor grammar in which some of it is written.* Now, some of the sweetest saints I have ever known use poor grammar. That, in itself, is not the point; blaming God for poor grammar is. Even when God gave His inspired word through such vessels as the unlearned and ignorant Peter, He did not use poor grammar.

Joseph F. Smith, sixth president of the Mormon church declared, "Joseph did not render the writing on the gold plates into the English language in his own style of language as many people believe, but every word and every letter was given to him by the gift and power of God."[5]

Joseph Smith himself declared, as late as 1841, in *History of the Church,* "I told the brethren that the Book of Mormon was the most correct of any book on earth."[6]

If the translated word was perfect, and if the 1830 *Book of Mormon* was perfect, why have the Mormons made some 4,000 changes in grammar, punctuation and word structure in the perfect *Book of Mormon*? These later Mormons, who were better educated, became increasingly embarrassed over grammatical errors in the *Book of Mormon*; so they made changes in later editions.

We have both a reproduction of the 1830 *Book of Mormon* and the current *Book of Mormon* and we can see the changes with our own eyes. Several students of Mormonism have made a count of the changes and the results have been noted in books, particularly by Arthur Budvarson, Marvin Cowan, and Jerald Tanner, as well as others.

Following are just a few examples of changes that have been made since the 1830 *Book of Mormon* (italics added):

1830 edition, page 52, "And are come forth out of the waters of Judah, which swear by the name of the Lord." 1963 edition, 1 Nephi 20:1, "And are come forth out of the waters of Judah, *or out of the waters of Baptism,* who swear by the name of the Lord."

1830 edition, page 303, "Yea, I know that he allotteth unto men, *yea, Decreeth unto them Decrees which are unalterable,* according to their wills." 1963 edition, Alma 29:4, "Yea, I know that he allotteth unto men according to their wills."

1830 edition, page 31, "Neither will the Lord God suffer that the Gentiles shall forever remain in the *state of awful woundedness.*" 1963 edition, 1 Nephi 13:32, "Neither will the Lord God suffer that the Gentiles shall forever remain in that *awful state of Blindness.*"

1830 edition, page 555, "...his sons and to his daughters, *which were not, or which* did not seek his destruction." 1963 edition, Ether 9:2, "...his sons and to his daughters *who* did not seek his destruction."

1830 edition, page 262, "And *it came to pass* that he began to plead for them, from that time forth; but it reviled him, saying: Art thou also possessed with the Devil? And *it came to pass* that they spit upon him." 1963 edition, Alma 14:7, "And he began to plead for them from that time forth; but they reviled him, saying: Art thou also possessed with the devil? And they spit upon him."

Another change from the 1830 *Book of Mormon* concerns Mosiah 21:28. King Benjamin had already died (Mosiah 6:5; p. 168) in the 1830 edition of the *Book of Mormon.* Apparently, Smith forgot this and in Mosiah 21:28, listed King Benjamin as being *alive!* Later, embarrassed Mormons changed the king's name to *King Mosiah* to remove the obvious contradiction!

One night I was sharing these facts with a fine, intelligent young graduate of Brigham Young University. This young man is something of a linguist having studied four or five languages. He served as a Mormon missionary to Lebanon and also in Switzerland. He now teaches Mormon priests in the Aaronic priesthood.

His answer? After groping for some time with various attempts which he saw fell far short, he said, "You know the difficulty of translating from one language to another. Then we have to take into account Joseph Smith's poor grammar and somewhat limited vocabulary. This may explain some of the problems."

As we can easily see, this in no way is an answer or solution to the problem. I was greatly surprised that this was the strongest answer my learned Mormon friend could come up with. If God did give Joseph Smith a letter-by-letter, word-for-word translation of His pure and perfect Word, surely He would have given it with correct grammar.

Interestingly enough, Joseph Smith's grammar was excellent as long as he copied verbatim from the King James. Why wouldn't it be excellent if he copied from "God's parchment" as he claimed?

Is the *Book of Mormon* a revelation from God or did Joseph Smith copy verses and chapters from the King James Bible and add material from his own imagination and from other available sources? Who really wrote the *Book of Mormon*?

If the Mormons claim that God directed Joseph Smith in translating the *Book of Mormon* they accuse God of using faulty grammar and of making other mistakes that later needed to be corrected. It does not seem wise, to say the least, to make this accusation about the Omniscient God of the Universe.

If we say Joseph Smith wrote the book, with its grammatical errors and other mistakes, we deny what Joseph Smith claimed, what the three witnesses claimed and what president Joseph F. Smith claimed. This would mean that Joseph Smith's testimony that the *Book of Mormon* is a letter-by-letter, word-by-word inerrant translation by the power of God is false. This accusation would irreparably jeopardize his claim that he was a prophet of God.

The Witnesses

In the front pages of the *Book of Mormon* is "The Testimony of Three Witnesses." The three witnesses, Oliver Cowdery, David Whitmer and Martin Harris, are said to have "seen the plates which contain the record... and... the engravings which are upon the plates." However, when questioned closely the witnesses said they never really saw the gold plates except when they were wrapped up or covered. They used terms like "vision," or "I saw them with the eye of faith."

Also, on the same page as the names of the three witnesses, is "The Testimony of Eight Witnesses." These witnesses were: Christian Whitmer, Jacob Whitmer, Peter Whitmer, Jr., John Whitmer, Hiram Page, Joseph Smith, Sr., Hyrum Smith and Samuel H. Smith. Of these eleven total witnesses, over half apostatized from the Mormon church. When I say *apostatized,* I don't mean they denied the church such as Peter, in a weak moment of fear, denied Christ, had his heart broken as any true Christian would, wept bitterly and within a few short hours sought his Saviour again. These witnesses departed from the Mormon church. Included were Cowdery, Whitmer and Harris and five of the eight witnesses. The three who remained were Smiths. (Even one or two of Joseph Smith's sons eventually left the LDS and affiliated with the Reorganized Church of Latter-day Saints.) Mormons claim that some of these witnesses came back to the church.

Some of these who apostatized even claimed they had revelations from God that Mormonism was false and that they should get out. Of course, Mormons don't accept their revelations, even though their visions sound as believable as those of Joseph Smith. We wonder why Mormons so readily accept the vision of a 14-year-old boy and so quickly reject the visions of several of these men.

David Whitmer, one of the original three witnesses, said God spoke to him in His own voice and told him to "separate myself from among the Latter-day Saints."[7]

According to *Doctrines of Salvation,* Cowdery and Harris returned to the church in their latter years and died in full fellowship.

Joseph Smith and other Mormon officials are on record as calling his three main witnesses "thieves and liars."[8] In *History of the Church* Joseph Smith said, "Such characters as ...David Whitmer, Oliver Cowdery, and Martin Harris, are too mean to mention, and we would like to have forgotten them."[9]

Can you *imagine* Jesus Christ calling His witnesses, Matthew, Mark, Luke, John and Paul, a bunch of liars and yet asking us to *believe* them as Joseph Smith has asked us to believe his witnesses to the *Book of Mormon*? Can you imagine Jesus Christ saying He'd like to forget the Gospel writers and Paul as Joseph Smith said he'd like to forget his main witnesses to the truth of the *Book of Mormon?*

There is one additional fact we feel we must include. Joseph Smith was tried and convicted of being a "glass-looker" (crystal-gazing fortune teller and treasure hunter) by a justice of the peace in Bainbridge, New York in 1826, six years after he was supposed to have had his first vision in 1820. The charge was made, according to the record of the trial, by one Peter G. Bridgemen, who said that Josiah Stowell had been deceived by Smith concerning finding lost property and gold treasures. He said Smith claimed to have powers by looking through a *stone*—the same process whereby Joseph Smith was able to translate the *Book of Mormon*, according to the three witnesses. A photograph of the original court record can be found in Jerald and Sandra Tanner's *Joseph Smith's 1826 Trial*.[10]

Footnotes

1. Robert Dick Wilson, *A Scientific Investigation of the Old Testament* (Chicago: Moody Press). Quoted by John R. Rice, *Our God-Breathed Book—The Bible* (Murfreesboro, Tenn.: Sword of the Lord Pub., 1969).

2. "Articles of Faith," *Pearl of Great Price.* Article #8, p. 60.

3. Orson Pratt, *Divine Authenticity of the Book of Mormon,* pp. 45–47. Quoted by Marvin Cowan, *Mormon Claims Answered* (Salt Lake City: Marvin Cowan Pub., 1975), pp. 21, 22

4. David Whitmer, *An Address to All Believers in Christ* (Richmond, Mo., 1887), p. 12; reprinted by Bales Bookstore, Searcy, Ark., 1960.

5. Whitmer, *An Address to All Believers in Christ,* p. 12.

6. Smith, *History of the Church,* vol. 4, p. 461.

7. Whitmer, *An Address to All Believers in Christ,* p. 27.

8. *Times and Seasons,* vol. 1, p. 81; *Elders Journal,* p. 59; *Senate Document* 189, pp. 6, 9.

9. Smith, *History of the Church,* vol. 3, p. 232.

10. Jerald and Sandra Tanner, *Joseph Smith's 1826 Trial* (Salt Lake City: Modern Microfilm Company, 1971).

CHAPTER FIVE

Joseph Smith Tested as a Translator

Martin Harris was one of the "three witnesses" to the *Book of Mormon.* He had been asked to mortgage his farm to help publish and distribute the *Book of Mormon.* As a precaution, Harris slipped off with a page or two of "reformed Egyptian" characters to Professor Charles Anthon, a renowned Egyptologist of Columbia University.

After examining the material, Anthon warned Harris that he was the victim of a fraud. The characters were not Egyptian hieroglyphics. However, Joseph Smith claimed in his revelation, *Pearl of Great Price,* that Anthon stated "that the translation was correct, more so than any he had before seen translated from the Egyptian. I then showed him those which were not yet translated, and he said that they were Egyptian, Chaldaic, Assyric, and Arabic; and he said they were true characters" (*Pearl of Great Price* 2:64).

53

Even if Anthon had not, in a letter, refuted the testimony of Joseph Smith, Smith's claim raises several problems. *First,* the reformed Egyptian was supposed to be a completely lost language "known to no man." Yet here is a man without any "divine revelation" who could read it! Not even Joseph Smith could do that!

Second, why did the papers have Chaldaic, Assyric and Arabic characters, if the gold plates were written only in reformed Egyptian?

Third, since this would have been the first and only translation from reformed Egyptian in over a thousand years, how could Anthon have said that it was the most correct translation from the Egyptian he had ever seen? How on earth could he have known if the translation into English was correct or not?

Fourth, Mormons claim this incident with Anthon fulfilled Isaiah 29:11,12: "And the vision of all is become unto you as the words of a book that is sealed, which men deliver to one that is learned, saying, Read this, I pray thee: and he saith, I cannot; for it is sealed: and the book is delivered to him that is not learned, saying, Read this, I pray thee: and he saith, I am not learned." If you read the passage carefully, you will see that the main subject is regarding the condition of the people at *that* time. It does not refer to a book at some future time.

Even so, Anthon never got hold of the complete book, only a paper or so with some characters on it. But Harris, according to Joseph Smith in *Pearl of Great Price,* said that Anthon claimed the translation was correct. He could only say this if he was able to *read* it. But Isaiah said the "learned man could *not* read the book because it was sealed."

There are several other problems, but this should be enough. God *never* contradicts Himself, not even in the *slightest detail* in fulfilling prophecy. This is how God told us to test the true from the false. And to refuse to make such a test would be to disobey God who told us to "believe not every spirit, but try [test] the spirits whether they are of God: because many false prophets are gone out into the world" (1 John 4:1). We are told that false prophets can perform miracles (lying wonders). We are also told that they appear as angels of light, ministers of righteousness.

Matthew 7:15 tells us, "Beware of false prophets, which come to you in sheep's clothing, but inwardly they are ravening wolves." If we love Jesus and His Word we can do no less than obey Him and apply the test to those who claim to be prophets of God. Terrible eternal loss will be the result to ourselves and countless others if we do not. If Joseph Smith could pass the test, we would be happy to accept him as a prophet of God. Unfortunately, he cannot.

The capstone to this whole story is a letter Professor Anthon wrote seven years later to E. D. Howe, February 17, 1834. "The whole story about my having pronounced the Mormon inscription to be reformed Egyptian hieroglyphics is *perfectly false....* I soon came to the conclusion that *it was all a trick—perhaps a hoax.... The paper contained anything else but Egyptian hieroglyphics.*"[1]

Perhaps the most damaging blow of all to Joseph Smith's credibility as a translator or prophet receiving revelations from God was an episode dating back to 1835. Joseph Smith purchased some Egyptian mummies and rolls of papyrus from Michael H. Chandler. Joseph Smith received revelations from God as to the meaning of the characters and sketches on the papyri. This translation, along with three drawings from the Egyptian papyri, he published as the "Book of Abraham" in the *Pearl of Great Price.* He claimed the first drawing, or "Facsimile no. 1," showed the idolatrous priest of Elkenah attempting to offer Abraham upon the altar as a sacrifice. The four jars underneath were idolatrous gods, etc. The bird pictured was the "Angel of the Lord."

Unfortunately for Joseph Smith, *this* time a scientific, analytical test could be made of his claims. This was a known language to Egyptologists, not "reformed Egyptian."

Bishop F. S. Spalding sent copies of this and several other facsimiles that Smith drew and translated from the Egyptian papyri to several of the foremost Egyptologists in the world.[2] They *all agreed* "embalming the dead" was the subject of the picture. *All* of them said that Joseph Smith's interpretation was *false,* and not a true translation of the facsimile or Egyptian hieroglyphics.

Then in 1967, a manuscript formerly believed to have been destroyed in the Chicago fire was unearthed. This was positively identified by the Mormons as the *original manuscript* from which Joseph Smith "translated" the information in the "Book of Abraham."

But Professor Dee Jay Nelson, prominent *Mormon* Egyptologist, after careful analysis of the papyri and the purported translations from the Egyptian to English by Joseph Smith, pronounced the "Book of Abraham" a false translation. Dee Jay Nelson used not only his own considerable linguistic ability but also the aid of a computer which showed that it was mathematically impossible for Joseph Smith to have translated so many words from so few Egyptian characters on so small a papyrus fragment (1,125 words from 46 characters).

This "original manuscript" for the "Book of Abraham" actually is an Egyptian funeral text from a few centuries before the birth of Christ, giving instructions to the embalmers. Joseph Smith's translation had this same text telling about Abraham and his life in Mesopotamia some 2,000 years earlier. Facsimiles nos. 1, 2 and 3, as well as other material from which Joseph Smith claimed to translate the "Book of Abraham" have been examined and shown to be mistranslations by Dee Jay Nelson and leading Egyptologists.[3]

Professor Nelson, a member of the Mormon priesthood, and his family resigned from the LDS Church December 8, 1975, as a result of this discovery. Professor Nelson, in a letter to R. L. Eardley of Billings, Montana, on February 15, 1976, stated: "The scientific world finds the Book of Abraham an insult to intelligence. Some of the most brilliant and qualified Egyptologists of our time have labeled it fraudulent upon the overwhelming evidence of the recently discovered Metropolitan-Joseph Smith Papyri. No truly qualified Egyptologist has yet supported it. We do not wish to be associated with a church which teaches lies and racial bigotry."

Perhaps at this time we should ask our Mormon friends if they can honestly and with all their hearts repose their eternal destiny on the credibility of Joseph Smith. As Mormons, this is what they are doing.

Footnotes

1. Letter from Professor Charles Anthon to E. D. Howe, February 17, 1834. Quoted by Tanner in *Mormonism, Shadow or Reality*, (Salt Lake City: Modern Microfilm Company, 1972), p. 105.

2. The Egyptologists were: Dr. A. H. Sayce, Oxford University; Dr. William M. F. Petrie, London University; Dr. A. C. Mace, Department of Egyptology, Metropolitan Museum of Art, New York; Dr. J. Peters, Director of the Babylonian Expedition of the University of Pennsylvania, 1888–1895; Dr. S. A. B. Mercer, Western Theological Seminary, Chicago; Dr. E. Meyer, University of Berlin; Dr. Baron V. Bissing, University of Munich.

3. Dee Jay Nelson, *The Joseph Smith Papyri*, Part 2, and *The Eye of Ra*. See also Tanner, *Mormonism, Shadow or Reality*, in their chapter "The Fall of the Book of Abraham."

CHAPTER SIX

History, Archeology, Anthropology and the Book of Mormon

It seems conclusive that any book truly inspired by God will be accurate historically and archeologically. Following is a very brief synopsis of the history of the *Book of Mormon* in this context.

History of the *Book of Mormon*

The *Book of Mormon* claims that a people called the Jaredites, refugees from the Tower of Babel, migrated to America about 2247 B.C. They occupied Central America until they were wiped out by internal strife. One survivor, the prophet Ether, recorded the history of the Jaredites on 24 metallic plates.

About 600 B.C. the two families of Lehi and Ishmael left Jerusalem, crossed the Pacific Ocean and landed in South America. Two sons of Lehi, Laman and Nephi, got in a fight and the people took sides and divided into two warring camps—the Lamanites and the Nephites. The Lamanites were cursed by the Lord because they were rebellious and against His commandments. Part of their curse included dark skins, which supposedly accounts for the origin of the American Indians.

God favored the Nephites who migrated to Central America about the time of Christ. Just after His crucifixion, Christ came to America and instituted baptism by immersion, the sacrament of bread and wine, the priesthood and gave many other teachings. Both Lamanites and Nephites were converted. Things were fairly smooth for about 200 years, then apostasy came. The term "Lamanite" then was placed on everyone who left the faith.

One hundred and fifty years later, the religious Nephites and irreligious Lamanites went to war again. In about A.D. 421 the Nephites were all killed, and the infidel Lamanites were left in control of the land. Columbus discovered them when he landed in 1492.

The Commander in Chief of the Nephites was a prophet and priest named Mormon. When he saw that they were defeated, he gathered the record of his predecessors and made an abbreviated history which he wrote on gold plates. He gave these gold plates to his son Moroni. Moroni hid them in a hill near Palmyra, New York, and about 1400 years later appeared as an angel to Joseph Smith and told him where to find the plates. In the box that held the plates was a large pair of spectacles, one glass called Urim, and the other Thummin. According to the three witnesses, by the help of these spectacles, urim and thummin or "interpreters," plus a "seerstone," Joseph Smith translated the hieroglyphics into English. The hieroglyphics were "reformed Egyptian" according to Joseph Smith, a language now "known to no man." In this fashion, the *Book of Mormon* was supposedly revealed.

Why were the plates buried in Palmyra, New York, aside from the fact that Joseph Smith lived in that area?

Well, as war began between the Lamanites and the Nephites, Mormon wrote a letter to the King of the Lamanites requesting him to meet the Nephites in the land of Cumorah, by a hill called Cumorah, "and there we would give him battle!" According to the story, Mormon hoped thereby to gain a military advantage, and apparently the Lamanite King and his forces were happy to oblige him! So, women and children marched over formidable mountains and through steaming jungles and across swift rivers for thousands of miles, by the hundreds of thousands, to fight a battle to the death in a place by a small insignificant hill most of them had never heard of!

One must admit this is quite a story. We cannot help but entertain the notion that this may have been the only way Joseph could think of to get the "gold plates" to his vicinity near Palmyra, New York.

Several remarkable problems need to be noted about this history.

The first problem concerns the rapid increase in population. According to the *Book of Mormon* in 30 years two *nations* grew from 28 people or less (see 2 Nephi 5:5,6,28). In this time the two nations (which at the greatest possible rate of increase could have numbered only several hundred, with the majority being women and children) divided and became fierce enemies called the Nephites and the Lamanites.

Nephites and Lamanites at various times "multiplied exceedingly, and spread upon the face of the land, and became exceeding rich" (Jarom 8), and "did multiply and spread... began to cover the face of the whole earth, from the sea south to the sea north, from the sea west to the sea east" (Helaman 3:8). They were "numerous almost, as it were the sands of the sea" (Mormon 1:7).

The second problem concerns the mighty cities the Nephites and Jaredites built. They "did build many mighty cities" (Ether 9:23; see also Alma 50,15). There are a least 38 names of cities mentioned in the *Book of Mormon*: Ammonihah, Bountiful, Gideon, Jacobugath, Jerusalem, Manti, Shem, Zarahemla, etc., all in the New World. However, not one of these city sites has ever been found in South or Central America.

By contrast a great amount of evidence has been uncovered concerning the ancient cities of the Mayas and Incas who occupied these areas! The historical or archeological support, which should be virtually overwhelming for such a civilization as the Mormons claim, simply does not exist. In fact, the opposite is true.

The third problem with the history of the Book of Mormon *is in the languages of the early people.* It is impossible that the languages of reformed Egyptian and Hebrew could have so completely disappeared if they were used so extensively in the Americas for hundreds of years.

Archeology and the *Book of Mormon*

I have before me now, as I type this manuscript, a beautiful 1961 edition of the *Book of Mormon*. Among the lovely pictures in the front of the book, is a picture of some murals depicting people, very un-Egyptian huts, water, boats, rowers, etc. The caption under the picture says, "Egyptian-like murals found on temple walls in Mexico." This is probably supposed to convey to the unwary reader's mind that this is a link in the chain of evidence for the background of the *Book of Mormon,* as it relates to the origin of the *Book of Mormon* people and their alleged presence in South and Central America. Actually this mural does not look any more Egyptian than it does Peruvian or African or Indian.

I have personally seen lavish, beautifully-illustrated books on archeology concerning South or Central America, which ardent Mormon missionaries sometimes use to *infer* archeological proof for the *Book of Mormon,* and so for Mormonism. Yet, there is not one knowledgeable archeologist, Mormon or non-Mormon, who will claim that there is any archeological proof to support the *Book of Mormon.* There is no evidence to support the existence of any of the cities Joseph Smith claims covered the Americas, apart from Joseph Smith's imagination.

Mormon authority John L. Sorenson, assistant professor of Anthropology and Sociology at Brigham Young University, commented, "We are of the opinion that Latter-day Saints ought to be satisfied with the truth and not try to improve upon it by gratuitous 'proofs' which are themselves based on untruth."[1] Professor Sorenson made his comments in rebutting *Book of Mormon Evidences in Ancient America,* by Dewey Farnsworth, one of the books seeking to establish evidence for the *Book of Mormon.*

Dr. Ross T. Christenson, a Mormon anthropologist, said, "The statement that the Book of Mormon has already been proved by archeology is misleading."[2] Remember, these statements are from *Mormon authorities* in the field of archeology.

In all of my research on Mormonism, I have not found one non-Mormon archeologist who gives any credence to the *Book of Mormon* history whatsoever. None of them uses it as a guide in archeological research in South and Central America. If any of my readers know of a bona fide, accredited, knowledgeable non-Mormon archeologist who does use the *Book of Mormon* as a guide, please send me his name and address.

A member of the Smithsonian Institute in Washington has commented, "The Smithsonian Institution has NEVER used the *Book of Mormon* IN ANY WAY as a scientific guide. Smithsonian archeologists see NO CONNECTION between the archeology of the New World and the subject matter of the Book."[3]

On the other hand, archeologists frequently discover proof

which utterly contradicts and demolishes the claims of the *Book of Mormon*. Though scientific research has demonstrated that the American continent was devoid of many domestic animals such as cattle, swine, horses, asses and certain other animals until the Europeans came to America, the *Book of Mormon* claims these were all here long before Christ.

With the exception of Brigham Young University the institutions of higher learning in America agree with the Smithsonian Institute that, "There is no evidence whatever of any migration from Israel to America, and likewise no evidence that pre-Columbian Indians had any knowledge of Christianity or the Bible."[4]

Anthropology and the *Book of Mormon*

Not only is there no archeological proof to support the *Book of Mormon* history of the vast civilizations that supposedly covered all of South and Central America, but anthropologists also deny the claims in the *Book of Mormon*.

Those who specialize in anthropology and genetics refute Joseph Smith's claim that the American Indians are descendants of the Israelites. Rather they say that the Indians resemble and are more closely related to peoples of eastern, central and northeastern Asia. These Asian people have a "Mongoloid Spot," a blue or blue-gray spot on their tailbones at birth. The American Indians also have a Mongoloid Spot. The Israelites, who are Semites, do not have it! American Indians are not Lamanite descendants of Israelites who migrated to America.

If the Indians are not descendants of the Israelites as the Mormons claim, then Joseph Smith and the *Book of Mormon* are in error, and certainly not inspired of God.

Faith and the *Book of Mormon*

This seems to be a good place to suggest to Mormons that they must deal honestly with hard evidence such as we have been pointing out. So many times I, as well as others, have brought these weighty and serious problems to the attention of Mormons only to be given a "testimony" about believing by faith. But there is never any attempt on their part to face or solve the problem with factual evidence.

Those of us who know the biblical Christ have a tremendous testimony as to the joy, new life, certainty and inner transformation our wonderful Saviour has given us. We have been saved, converted, born again, washed clean from our sins by the blood of Christ. We have been made children of God, given eternal life at a definite point in time and we *know* it. However, if strong evidence were produced that Christ had been born in Athens instead of Bethlehem, or that the Bible was totally false on a number of historical and archeological points or that many of the biblical prophecies had failed, then it would be exceedingly foolish of us to answer with our "testimony" as to how the Holy Spirit had convinced us of the truth of the Bible.

Faith cannot operate without some intellectual content. God never asks for blind faith, only the devil does that. The God of biblical truth is also the God of historical and archeological truth, and the one never contradicts the other in fact.

God says, "Faith cometh by hearing, and hearing by the word of God" (Rom. 10:17). But for this to be valid, one must first have confidence that the Bible really is the Word of God. True, this confidence is established in the willing heart by the Holy Spirit. He also reveals to the seeker the desolate fact that he is a *lost* sinner, and the sublime and wonderful fact that Christ is the one and only Saviour. However, even the Holy Spirit does not do this without some factual intellectual content. This is why Jesus and the disciples often said, referring to prophecies made centuries before, "This is that which the prophet said..." Fulfilled prophecy, historical and archeological trustworthiness, the resurrection of Christ, and other evidence, all furnish a solid foundation from which true faith can be launched. One is not bludgeoned into believing by fact alone, much room is left for faith.

Mormon friends question that the Bible teaches that we can be saved by faith alone without works; however, they hastily retreat into a faith-alone shelter when facts threaten to destroy the very fabric of Mormonism. There is no way that "testimony" can clear up contradictions or turn that which is false into that which is true.

In Summary

God asks for faith which rests on solid facts and proven promises.

Take another look at the Mormon cities that supposedly flourished in South and Central America. Scores of Bible cities have been verified easily. Some of these were as old as, and others much older than, many of the Mormon cities named in the *Book of Mormon*—cities and city-states like Ur of the Chaldees, Jerusalem, Nineveh, the Hittite city-kingdom, etc. Archeologists continue to unearth cities the Scriptures tell about.

The Bible has been found, even by unbelievers, to be geographically and archeologically accurate. Archeologists— believers and unbelievers—use the Bible as a guide and find it extremely reliable in research in Bible lands.

If we are supposed to trust a book to guide us in truths about a world we have not yet seen, we would surely expect to find it accurate and trustworthy, historically and geographically, in matters about the world we have seen. The Bible meets this requirement. The *Book of Mormon* does not.

Footnotes

1. John L. Sorenson in a review of the Dewey Farnsworth book.
2. Ross T. Christensen, Mormon Anthropologist, *U.A.S. Newsletter,* No. 64 (Provo, Utah: University Archeological Society, January 30, 1960), p. 3.
3. Quoted from Tanner, *Mormonism, Shadow or Reality* (Salt Lake City: Modern Microfilm Company, 1975), p. 97.
4. Dr. Frank H. H. Roberts, Jr., Director of the Bureau of American Ethnology at the Smithsonian Institute. Quoted by Marvin W. Cowan, *Mormon Claims Answered,* published by Marvin W. Cowan, 1975.

CHAPTER SEVEN

The Fatal Flaw

Is the God of Mormonism the God of the Bible? Is the Christ of Mormonism the Christ of the Bible?

Ephesians 4:15 cautions us to be "speaking the truth in love," and I will endeavor, as God enables, to do just that. God loves Mormons and non-Mormons and Christ died for both. He is looking for honest, searching hearts wherever He may find them.

The very heart of any position claiming to be Christian is what it teaches about God and about Jesus Christ. If one has wrong views about God, then it is easy for wrong doctrine to flow from this fatal flaw.

Let us then kindly and objectively see what Mormonism teaches about God and what the Bible teaches about God. Is the God of Mormonism the God of the Bible?

The God of the Mormons

The heart, the very quintessence of Mormon doctrine, the

embryo from which Mormonism was spawned, the sustenance which nourishes it, and the goal for which earnest Mormons strive is their belief in God:

"We believe in a God who is Himself progressive, whose majesty is intelligence; whose perfection consists in eternal advancement—a Being who has *attained* His exalted state by a path which now His children are permitted to follow, whose glory it is their heritage to share. In spite of the opposition of the sects, in face of direct charges of blasphemy, the Church proclaims the eternal truth, '*As man is, God once was: as God is, man may be*' [1] (italics added).

Here, in the *Articles of Faith,* one of Mormonism's most treasured books, we have the hub of their teaching. What is it? God was once a man and He earned or attained or progressed His way to being God. Man, in turn, may also earn, attain or progress his way into being a God. This is one of the fundamental reasons for the good works Mormons do, for their church and temple work.

Lest someone still thinks this is not what Mormonism teaches, let me again quote, from their own sources, none other than Prophet Joseph Smith: "God himself was once as we are now, and is an exalted man, and sits enthroned in yonder heavens!....I am going to tell you *how God came to be God.* We have imagined and supposed that God was God from all eternity. I will refute that idea, and take away the veil, so that you may see." [2]

From still another Mormon source: "Mormon prophets have continuously taught the sublime truth that God the Eternal Father was once a mortal man who passed through a school of earth life similar to that through which we are now passing. Remember that God our Heavenly Father was perhaps once a child, and mortal like we are, and rose step by step in the scale of progress in the school of advancement." [3]

Do we now understand clearly what Mormonism teaches about God and about man? Prophet Smith and his followers teach that God was not always God, and that He had to earn, progress, work, attain His way into being God. He was once a man just like us before He ever became God. We too may work, progress, earn and attain our way to being a god. "As man is, God once was; as God is, man may be."

The God of the Bible

The Bible is the original revelation about God, preceding the *Book of Mormon* by many long centuries. In any conflict of views the Bible must have precedence over the *Book of Mormon* as well as any other of the sacred books or teachings of Mormonism.

Now let's compare the God of the Bible with the God of Mormonism. First of all, there has never been, there is not now, and there never will be any but the one true and only God.

God's Word declares in 1 Corinthians 8:5,6, "For though there be that are *called* gods, whether in heaven or in earth, (as there be gods many, and lords many) but to us there is but *one God*" (italics added). In this verse the apostle Paul is referring to pagan polytheism, which included many gods and idols. He declares emphatically that there is only one God, the God known to us, true believers in Christ.

Even more devastating to Mormonism, however, is the word of God in Isaiah 43:10, "Ye are my witnesses, saith the Lord, and my servant whom I have chosen; that ye may know and believe me, and understand that I am he: *before me there was no God formed, neither shall there be after me!*" (italics added).

Look carefully also, at Isaiah 44:6. "Thus saith the Lord the King of Israel, and his redeemer the Lord of hosts; I am the *first,* and I am the *last*; and beside me there is *no* God" (italics added).

Continue on to Isaiah 46:9. "Remember the former things of old: for I am God, and there is *none else*; I am God, and there is *none like me*" (italics added).

69

Now it is clear that God declares that He is the *one* and *only* true God, in this universe or any other, in this world or any other, on this planet or any other. There *is* no other God. This is the very same God of Genesis 1:1, "In the beginning God created the heaven and the earth." Genesis 1:16 tells us He made the stars and Genesis 2:1 declares, "Thus the heavens and the earth were finished, and all the host of them."

God made all possible worlds, universes, planets, stars and He is the one and only God of them all. There are *no* other Gods in existence anywhere. He *alone* is the one and only true God. There was no God before Him, there is no other God now, and *there never will be any other god.* He is the first and the last.

One of the primary names of God, *Jehovah,* means in essence, self-existent one; one who has life originally, permanently, and forever, within Himself.

God, then, was *never* a man, *never* mortal, but was *always* God. He is not now an "exalted man," as Mormonism claims. God explicitly declares, "For I am God, and not man" (Hos. 11:9).

Because God plainly declared in Isaiah 43:10 that there would be no God after Him, *no man will ever now, or in the future, or in eternity, become a god.* Therefore the Mormon creed, their main thrust, "As man is, God once was; as God is, man may be," is totally untrue to the Bible. It is not of God. "*Before* me there was no God formed, neither shall there be *after* me" (Isa. 43:10; italics added).

God did not attain His way to being God and He was never a man. He always was God. Psalm 90:2 says, "Before the mountains were brought forth, or ever thou hadst formed the earth and the world, even from everlasting to everlasting, thou art God."

Now we all know that everlasting means without end, enduring forever. Then what does, "*from* everlasting," mean? Exactly the same, but applied to the past. God was God from everlasting past, just as He alone is God now, and just as He alone will be God in the everlasting, non-ending future!

This is utterly contrary to the Mormon teaching that "as man is, God once was; as God is, man may be." We cannot have it both ways. Either we believe this or we believe the Bible.

Mormonism says God was once man. God's Word says God was always God, never man, from everlasting, eternity past.

Mormonism says God had a beginning. God's Word says He did not.

Mormonism says there are many gods and will be more. God's Word says there never has been, is not now and never will be any other God.

Mormonism says man can become a god. God's Word says there will never be any other God. Christianity, biblically and historically, has always been monotheistic, believing in one God. Paganism, biblically and historically, has always been polytheistic, believing in more than one God. Neither the Old Testament nor the New Testament, nor Jesus, nor His disciples, nor early Christians, as can be proven from church history, ever taught that there was more than one God.

Thus far in this chapter, we have contrasted the God of Mormonism with the God of the Bible. We have discovered that the God of the Mormons and the God of the Bible seem to have little in common. To be sure, Mormons refer to God in some biblical terms which cloak the glaring and fatal differences from the unwary; but when they call their God "eternal" they have a totally different meaning than the Bible does. When Mormon writings give glowing accounts of "the eternal God, mighty creator, everlasting Father," and so on, these wonderful words do not mean what they seem to say. They have no true relation to the one true God of the Bible whose very name as revealed to Moses is "I AM," underlying the fact that God always was, is now, and forever shall be the one and only God!

In the second part of this discussion on the fatal flaw we ask another question: *Is the Christ of Mormonism the Christ of the Bible?*

The Christ

As the Mormons have done with God, so have they done with Jesus Christ. The Bible teaches that Jesus Christ is God the Son. God came down to earth in human flesh to shed His blood for our sins and conquer death for us by His bodily resurrection.

The Mormons teach that Jesus Christ is a God named *Jehovah,* another God, different from God the Father whose name is *Elohim.* The Bible uses these names interchangeably as applied to the one true God and Jesus Christ, as indicated in Deuteronomy 6:4, "The Lord [Jehovah] our God [Elohim] is one Lord [Jehovah]." However, the Mormons' teaching concerning Jesus Christ is that "Christ the Word, the Firstborn, had of course *attained* unto the status of Godhood while yet in pre-existence."[4]

Contrary to Mormon teaching, Christ always was, is now and forever shall be, God. He did *not attain* to being God for there was *never* a time when He was *not* God.

Of course, Christ had a human beginning insofar as becoming a man through the virgin birth. However, consider Isaiah 9:6: "For unto us a child is born, unto us a son is given [a clear and universally acknowledged prophecy of the coming Christ]: and the government shall be upon his shoulder: and his name shall be called Wonderful, Counsellor, *The mighty God, The everlasting Father,* The Prince of Peace" (italics added). Here God's Word calls Jesus Christ "God, The everlasting Father." (See also Jer. 32:18.)

That's right, Jesus Christ is that one, true and eternal God, manifested in the flesh (see John 1:1). Christ is called God numerous times: "My Lord and my God" (John 20:28); "But unto the Son he saith, Thy throne, O God, is for ever and ever"

(Heb. 1:8). Since God declared in Isaiah 43:10 (and in numerous other places) that He is the one and *only* God, and that there will *never* be another. Jesus Christ, then, is either a false god and no god at all, or He is that one true God revealed in the flesh as the Son of God.

Another prophecy concerning Jesus Christ the God-man, Micah 5:2, "But thou, Bethlehem Ephratah, though thou be little among the thousands of Judah, yet out of thee shall he come forth unto me that is to be ruler in Israel; whose goings forth have been from of old, from everlasting." This "from everlasting" definitely means from all eternity past, without any beginning, as we have already discovered.

John 1:1 states, "In the beginning was the Word, and the Word was with God, and the Word was God." (Later in John 1:14 we see that "The Word was made flesh and dwelt among us," making Christ and the Word synonymous.) John 1:1 teaches us that Christ was the Word and that He was with God and that He *was* (not became) God. Again, here in the first verse of John's Gospel, we see that God was God from the beginning (which here has the sense of meaning "from all time") and so Jesus Christ was God from the beginning, from all time!

Jesus Christ accepted worship as God on many occasions because He was God. For example, "And as they went to tell his disciples, behold Jesus met them, saying, All hail. And they came and held him by the feet, and worshipped Him" (Matt. 28:9).

Now God has absolutely forbidden the worship of any other god, in biblical passages such as Exodus 34:14, "For thou shalt worship no other god; for the Lord, whose name is Jealous, is a jealous God." The fact that Jesus permitted, encouraged and accepted worship identified Him as God, and there is only one God who has been and will be God, "from everlasting to everlasting."

Not only is the God of Mormonism not the God of the Bible,

73

but we also have to affirm that the Christ of Mormonism is not the Christ of the Bible.

The Mormon's teaching about God and Jesus Christ lead us to still more error in doctrine—the doctrine of salvation.

The Way to Salvation

The Mormon belief that "as man is, God once was: as God is, man may be" lends itself to unsaved man's deception that he can somehow earn his salvation, or help earn it. This belief fosters the idea that man can become one of God's sheep by ignoring his sin nature and acting like a sheep, which is as futile as a pig acting like a sheep in order to become a sheep.

We need to have our nature changed by the new birth, and thus receive a new nature: "For all have sinned, and come short of the glory of God" (Rom. 3:23). No church, baptism or great amount of good works can change our nature or pay for past sins. We must turn to Jesus *alone* for salvation, knowing that His shed blood will cleanse us from all sin. Simultaneously, as we call believingly on Him, He will enter our life to change our nature from within. This makes us true children of God. "Nothing in our hands we bring, simply to His Cross we cling."

Salvation is ours through the grace of God: "For by grace are ye saved through faith; and that not of yourselves: it is the gift of God: not of works, lest any man should boast" (Eph. 2:8,9).

The *grace of God* of which Mormons sometimes write is far removed from the grace of God of which the Bible speaks. The Mormon concept of grace consists in part of doing church, temple and religious good works and so making oneself *worthy* of the grace of God. Biblical grace is extended freely to the *totally undeserving,* as in the case of the thief on the cross (see Luke 23:39-43). As we call on Christ, undeservingly but believingly, He responds with instant salvation. Then as He enters our lives and makes us children of God, our lives are changed by Christ from within. We receive a new nature, new desires, new love and new power. Behold the mad murderer, Saul, who became the magnificent missionary, Paul, after one vital encounter with the risen Christ on the road to Damascus.

In Summary

One of the most puzzling things for Christians to understand and accept is that Mormon friends will use the same terminology but mean something entirely different.

So many Christians, tragically, never look behind the words of sincere Mormon friends who declare to them that they have accepted Christ as their Saviour, and love Him. They say they are depending on Him for their salvation. Of course, they may add, they have a little more light, truth, or a higher salvation, since they are Mormons and in the Mormon church!

Mormons use the name "Christ," but in using the word they are thinking of someone or something entirely different, unless they don't know Mormon doctrine. In that case he is not a Mormon at all, except in name. If he truly accepts the Christ of the Bible, he will soon thirst for an oasis of true Christians, and will leave the Mormon church.

In any event, if you have a Mormon friend, love him and be patient with him as you would want him to be with you and as Christ is with us. However, probe gently but carefully into his testimony until you discover which Christ he is trusting, and whether or not he believes there is more than one God.

A true Mormon must believe Mormon scriptures such as Joseph Smith's *Pearl of Great Price*: "And the Gods ordered, saying: Let the waters under the heaven be gathered together unto one place, and let the earth come up dry; and it was so as they ordered; And the Gods pronounced the dry land, earth; and the gathering together of the waters, pronounced they, great waters; and the Gods saw that they were obeyed" (Abraham 4:9,10).

To believe that other *gods* even exist is polytheistic

paganism, not Christianity. It is a denial of the Word of God. We really must choose, as must our Mormon friends, to believe either the biblical God or Mormonism's gods. They are mutually exclusive.

The intensely religious, but lost, Pharisees made a fatal error. They worshiped God under His correct name, did many good works for Him, belonged to the worship system God had established, prayed much, gave much, prospered much, were extremely religious, and had priests in their church. The Pharisees appeared as angels of light and ministers of righteousness and really believed themselves to be right, to be in the one true "church" serving God, but they were tragically wrong. They never truly accepted Jesus Christ as God and remained forever lost, with the exception of a few who trusted Jesus.

In Matthew 24:23,24, our Lord spoke the awesome words: "Then if any man shall say unto you, Lo, here is Christ, or, there; believe it not. For there shall arise false Christs, and false prophets, and shall show great signs and wonders; insomuch that, if it were possible, they shall deceive the very elect."

Facts alone can never open eyes. However the Holy Spirit does use facts, and this is written in the love of Christ that He may, through these facts, open many eyes to deliverance and salvation.

Footnotes

1. James E. Talmage, A Study of the *Articles of Faith* (Salt Lake City: The Church of Jesus Christ of Latter-day Saints, 1952), p. 430.

2. Joseph Fielding Smith, comp., *Teachings of Prophet Joseph Smith* (Salt Lake City: Deseret News Press, 1958), p. 345.

3. Milton R. Hunter, *The Gospel Through the Ages* (Salt Lake City: Deseret Book Co., 1945), p. 104.

4. B. R. McConkie, *What the Mormons Think of Christ* (tract) (Salt Lake City: Deseret News Press), p. 36.

CHAPTER EIGHT

Contradictions Concerning the Person of God

The Bible is the foundation of what God had to say to man. When there is a contradiction between what the Bible teaches and what the *Book of Mormon* or any Mormon books teach, the Bible must be given preeminence.

We do not intend to try to give in this book an exhaustive exposition of the many contradictions between the Bible and the various books of Mormon doctrine. If you are anxious to pursue the subject we recommend *Mormonism, Shadow or Reality,* by Jerald and Sandra Tanner. This 600-page volume contains an open challenge to any scholar or group of scholars to try to answer, point by point, the contradictions it reveals.

However, we do want to take a close look at some of the contradictions between the Bible and Mormon teachings concerning the doctrine of God. We also will reveal contradictions between "inspired" Mormon books written by Joseph Smith and the *Book of Mormon* concerning the person of God.

Mormons Believe There Are Many Gods

Mormonism denies that there is *one* God. While the *Book of Mormon* seems to teach the doctrine of the trinity as Christians believe it, other teachings of Joseph Smith say there are many gods.

The Scriptures say: "But to us there is but one God" (1 Cor. 8:6; see also vv. 4,5); "Before me there was no God formed, neither shall there be after me" (Isa. 43:10); "I am God, and there is none else" (Isa. 45:22). (See also Deut. 4:35; 32:39; 2 Sam. 7:22; Ps. 86:10.)

The *Book of Mormon* says: "... of the Father, and of the Son, and of the Holy Ghost, which is one God, without end" (2 Nephi 31:21). Alma 11:26-31 quotes Amulek as answering Zeezrom that there is only *one* God, and Amulek is described as a man filled with the Spirit of the Lord. Alma 11:22 and Mosiah 15:4,5, also speak of the Father and Son as being one God.

However, in *Doctrine and Covenants,* we read that Abraham, Isaac and Jacob "have entered into their exaltation, according to the promises, and sit upon thrones, and are not angels but are gods" (132:37). In the *Pearl of Great Price,* Joseph Smith wrote, "So the Gods went down to organize man in their own image, in the image of the Gods to form they him, male and female, to form they them" (Abraham 4:27). The Bible and the *Book of Mormon* both declare that there is *one* God but *Doctrine and Covenants* and the *Pearl of Great Price* declare that there are many gods.

The statement of the three witnesses in the front of the *Book of Mormon* includes this sentence: "And the honor be to the Father, and to the Son, and to the Holy Ghost, which is one God." Contrast this with a statement from the *Teachings of Prophet Joseph Smith* in which Joseph Smith says, "In the beginning, the head of the gods called a council of the gods." Also in one version of his first vision he claims that the Father and Son appeared to him as two different beings with two different literal bodies. Some Mormon friends of mine use this as a basis for their belief that God the Father and God the Son are two different Gods. This belief is contrary to the Bible and the *Book of Mormon*.

Still more confusing to anyone studying the doctrine of God in Mormon teachings are contradictions that can be found *in the same book*. For one example, the *Pearl of Great Price* says in Moses 2:9,10: "And I, God, said: Let the waters under the heaven be gathered together unto one place, and it was so; and I, God, said: Let there be dry land; and it was so. And I, God, called the dry land Earth; and the gathering together of the waters, called I the Sea; and I God saw that all things which I had made were good." But in Abraham 4:9,10 the *Pearl of Great Price* reads: "And the Gods ordered, saying: Let the waters under the heaven be gathered together unto one place, and let the earth come up dry; and it was so as they ordered; and the Gods pronounced the dry land, earth; and the gathering together of the waters, pronounced they, great waters; and the Gods saw that they were obeyed."

Mormons Believe God Is an Exalted Man

We have mentioned that Mormons teach that God was once a man before He progressed to being God. According to their teaching, God is now an exalted man, and man himself may become a God.

The Scriptures teach us: "Before the mountains were brought forth, or ever thou hadst formed the earth and the world, even from everlasting to everlasting [that's forever past, forever future], thou art God" (Ps. 90:2); there is "no variableness, neither shadow of turning" with God (Jas. 1:17); "For I am the Lord, I change not" (Mal. 3:6); "In the beginning God..." (Gen. 1:1); "Now unto the King eternal, immortal, invisible..." (1 Tim. 1:17).

The *Book of Mormon* says, "For do we not read that God is the same yesterday, today, and forever, and in him there is no variableness neither shadow of changing?" (Mormon 9:9); "For I know that God is not a partial God, neither a changeable being; but he is unchangeable from all eternity to all eternity" (Moroni 8:18); "God... being from everlasting to everlasting" (Moroni 7:22).

The *Pearl of Great Price* says, "Behold, I am the Lord God Almighty, and Endless is my name, for I am without beginning of days or end of years" (Moses 1:3).

With these definite, clear assertions from the Bible, the *Book of Mormon* and the *Pearl of Great Price,* that God had no beginning, that He was always God, and that He is an unchangeable being, what a shock it is to encounter the following from prophet Joseph Smith and prophet Brigham Young: "How God came to be God...refuting the idea that He was God from all eternity";[1] "First God himself, who sits enselves";[2] "Adam was God, our eternal Father" (Brigham Young, selves"[2] "Adam was God, our eternal Father" (Brigham Young, in *Journal of Joseph Lee Robinson*).

God's answer to this untruth is, "For I am God, and not man" (Hos. 11:9).

One of the problems Mormons have with the claim that God was once a man is this: If God was once a man *before* He became God then man, in effect, becomes the creator or at least the evolving forerunner of God, instead of God creating man. In conversations with Mormon friends, I have pointed this out and they have quickly denied that such is the case. Yet it is an obvious fact. If we follow this line of reasoning Mormons often say that this man who became God really had another God for a Father, and perhaps even a Mother God. The Mormons usually get increasingly vague at this point.

Mormons Believe God Has a Physical Body

In keeping with their doctrine that God is an exalted man, Mormons and Mormon teaching claim that God has a visible, material body. Biblical verses like Exodus 33:11 are used in support of this doctrine, "And the Lord spake unto Moses, face to face, as a man speaketh unto his friend."

God has been seen in anthropomorphic or theophanic appearances, as a man, angel, etc., and as incarnate in Christ. He has never been seen in His divine essence. Exodus 33 continues in verse 20, "And he said, Thou canst not see my face: for there shall no man see me, and live." John 1:18 adds, "No man hath seen God at any time; the only begotten Son, which is in the bosom of the Father, he hath declared him."

After His resurrection, Jesus appeared to His disciples and said, "Behold my hands and my feet, that it is myself: handle me and see; for a spirit hath not flesh and bones, as ye see me have" (Luke 24:39). Jesus here confirmed that a spirit cannot be seen or touched.

"God is a Spirit" (John 4:24)—not *has* a Spirit, but *is* a Spirit. A spirit is invisible as the Bible says God is, and does not have a body of flesh and bone. It is true that we find in Scripture, references to the mouth, arms, eyes, ears, face and hands of God. However, these references are symbolic, not literal. God uses them to communicate truth to us that we can understand.

If our Mormon friends insist on taking every description of God as literal they may wind up with a very strange God. Deuteronomy 4:24 says, "For the Lord thy God is a consuming fire," the blast-furnace God. Jeremiah 23:24 says, "Do not I fill heaven and earth? saith the Lord." If God were flesh and bone, this might make it a little uncomfortable for the rest of us! In Jeremiah 2:13, God calls Himself the "fountain of living waters." Psalm 91:4, "He shall cover thee with his feathers, and under his wings shalt thou trust." Surely this verse cannot be taken literally, for our wonderful God is not a chicken or a bird.

The Mormon claim that God is an exalted man and has a physical body has carried the Mormons to the brink of blasphemy. Brigham Young, in *Journal of Discourses* says, "Adam...is our father and our God and the only God with whom we have to do." Again he says, "Jesus Christ was not begotten by the Holy Ghost."[3]

Brigham Young went on to say that the Father of Jesus was the first of the human family—Adam, the same character that was in the Garden of Eden!

The Bible says, "For that which is conceived in her is of the Holy Ghost" (Matt. 1:20).

Certainly, the fact that man has a body of flesh and bone does not mean that God is made of the same material, especially when He clearly teaches that He is not. To believe literally that man is made in the image of God could be most confusing. Would God look like a man or a woman? Which race would He resemble in facial characteristics? We are made in the image of God in that we have self-awareness, abstract reasoning power, a spiritual nature and a God-awareness.

In Summary

It seems undeniable that there really are contradictions between the teachings of the Bible and the teachings of the *Book of Mormon* and Mormon prophets and teachers. It also seems undeniable that Mormon books and prophets contradict each other.

Mormon friends have often said to us, "You are taking what Joseph Smith (or whoever) said out of context!"

Of course, taking things out of context is a problem for all of us, isn't it? Obviously I cannot quote entire passages, chapters or volumes; there would not be enough space. That is why I have carefully listed the quotations, pages, etc., and quoted mostly from the Mormons' own teachings, so that they may read what is said in context for themselves. I want them to see that the portions I have quoted accurately reflect the teaching of the context as a whole.

Any book that claims to be the Word of God must be tested by the Bible. There is no other book inspired by the Holy Spirit. The Bible is the one and only Word of God and it is enough.

Footnotes

1. Smith, *Teachings of Prophet Joseph Smith,* p. 345.
2. Smith, *Times and Seasons,* vol. 5, pp. 613, 614.
3. Young, *Journal of Discourses,* vol. 1, pp. 50, 51.

CHAPTER NINE

Priesthood and Genealogies

The Mormons have done exactly what Jesus Christ said *not* to do. They have put "new wine in old bottles!" They have wed grace to law and made Christianity into a Jewish sect. They have resurrected what Christ buried. They have figuratively "sewn up" the veil that Christ, as our High Priest, rent forever to provide for us free access into the Holy of Holies.

How have they done this? Why have they done this? In their attempt to justify their existence and lend authority to their beliefs, and in their attempt to prove that they are the "one true church" they have restored the distinctively Jewish, Old Testament priesthood, and have turned again to the study and preserving of genealogies. The Mormon church claims that only those who hold the priesthood in the Mormon church have the authority to administer the ordinances of the gospel. Therefore, they believe there is no true salvation, no access to the "highest" heaven outside of the Mormon church. All ordinances performed by any other church are in vain.

Genealogies once had a firm connection with the priesthood

as to verifying qualifications for the priesthood. Mormons have built up the most elaborate genealogical system in the world.

The Aaronic Priesthood

The lesser of the two priesthood organizations in the Mormon church is the Aaronic or Levitical priesthood. This Aaronic priesthood was supposedly restored when John the Baptist appeared to Joseph Smith and Oliver Cowdery May 15, 1829, and conferred the Aaronic priesthood on them. Read the account in *Pearl of Great Price,* Joseph Smith 2:68-73.

Since Oliver Cowdery later defected from the LDS church and was even called a liar by Joseph Smith and others, I would say that his testimony of the restoration of the Aaronic priesthood is a little suspect, to say the least. (Both Marvin Cowan and Jerald Tanner in their respective books, *Mormon Claims Answered* and *Mormonism, Shadow or Reality,* quote several Mormon writers who totally contradict the claims of the restored Aaronic priesthood.)

The order of the Aaronic priesthood in the Mormon church includes *deacons,* boys 12 to 15 years of age; *teachers,* boys 15 to 18; and *priests,* boys 18 to 20 years of age.

The Melchizedek Priesthood

According to Talmage, sometime after the Aaronic priesthood was conferred in 1829, Peter, James and John also conferred the Melchizedek priesthood on Joseph Smith and Oliver Cowdery.[1] Mormon historian B. H. Roberts admits that "There is no definite account of the event [the conferring of the Melchizedek priesthood on Joseph Smith and Oliver Cowdery] in the history of the prophet Joseph, or, for matter of that, in any of our annals."[2]

This higher order of the two Mormon priesthoods is "called the Melchizedek Priesthood... because Melchizedek was such a great high priest" (*Doctrine and Covenants* 107:2). (See Gen.

14:18; Ps. 110:4; Heb. 5:6; 6:20; 7:1.) The officers of this priesthood include *elders, seventies,* and *high priests.* The Mormons believe that, "like God himself, the Melchizedek Priesthood is eternal and everlasting in nature." It is "an everlasting principle, and existed with God from eternity, and will to eternity, without beginning of days or end of years."[3]

Long years before God ever established the priesthood as a continuing office through Aaron, the Scriptures tell of a man named Melchizedek (Gen. 14). Melchizedek was without recorded beginning or ending and was a high priest and king. In these things he was a picture of the Lord Jesus Christ, our everlasting God (Isa. 9:6), High Priest, and King of kings.

After the introduction of this one man, Melchizedek, there was no other Melchizedek priesthood ordained of God for centuries. No man, after Melchizedek, held this office until Jesus came and fulfilled the picture that Melchizedek and his priesthood portrayed. When Jesus came He alone was declared to be a "priest for ever after the order of Melchizedek" (Heb. 7:21). Jesus, "because he continueth ever, hath an unchangeable priesthood" (Heb. 7:24). According to Greek scholars like Robertson and Thayer, *unchangeable* means "untransferable." Jesus alone, for all time, is our Melchizedek priest. For anyone to claim to be a Melchizedek priest today seems exceedingly unwise. Read Hebrews 7.

One look at the Mormon church with its restored Aaronic and Melchizedek priesthoods should convince anyone who is at all acquainted with the New Testament church that the Mormons have restored too much! They restored what was never there! There were no officers such as Aaronic or Melchizedek priests, seventies, high priests, etc., in the New Testament church. Nevertheless, this is the structure upon which the LDS church is built—the authority of the restored Aaronic and Melchizedek priesthoods, found only in the Mormon church.

The office of deacon, as the New Testament describes

it, should be sought by those who are "the husbands of one wife, ruling their children and their own houses well" (1 Tim. 3:12). Can a 12-year-old boy qualify for deacon under this description?

God commanded that the priests were to come through the tribe of Levi, and directly through Aaron and his sons and descendants. Yet most Mormons claim to be either from the tribes of Ephraim or Manasseh—the wrong tribes!

One of the highest duties of the priests in the Old Testament was to offer blood sacrifices. Mormon priests do not. If this is a restoration of the priesthood, why don't they?

Genealogies

The real purpose of all Mormon genealogical work is to provide information for baptizing for the dead, proxy sealing ordinances (an ordinance whereby husbands and wives are sealed together in the marriage union for time and eternity), and ordination and endowments for dead relatives to help save or exalt them. Thus Mormons search out the names of the dead through genealogical research and proceed to be baptized in their behalf. President Joseph Fielding Smith said, "The greatest commandment given us, and made obligatory, is the temple work in our own behalf and in behalf of our dead."[4]

The Mormon church keeps microfilms of all this genealogical work in large tunnels drilled in a granite mountain in Little Cottonwood Canyon, southeast of Salt Lake City. These genealogies go back for centuries. Forty-five million people have already been baptized by proxy. In 1975 alone more than three million were baptized in 16 Mormon temples. Thirteen camera crews in this country and 67 other camera crews around the world labor to add microfilmed information about the dead to this mass. Over 120 million dollars have been spent in this effort.

In 1966 "The total microfilm load included 579,679,800 pages of documents. There were more than 5 billion names in the files—the church puts about 4 million dollars a year into the Genealogical Society. It has 575 employees and is run by a board which includes two Apostles."[5]

Friends, all of you who are bound by priests and genealogies, read carefully and joyfully. I have good news for you!

Good-bye Sacrifices, Priests and Genealogies

Good news! Wonderful news! No more sacrifice has to be offered for our sins. Jesus offered "one sacrifice for sins forever" (Heb. 10:12), and thereby did away with the need for any other sacrifice.

Old Testament priests had as their chief function the offering of blood sacrifices as an atonement for sin (see Lev. 9:1,2). All their sacrifices symbolized the day when Christ, the Lamb of God, would shed His blood for our sins. When Jesus died on the cross the picture was fulfilled and the need for sacrifices, and therefore the need for priests, was done away with.

When my friend John was sharing his Mormon doctrine with me, he frequently claimed that all churches were false except the Mormon church. One reason for this is that we had no authority because we had no official priesthood, no apostles or prophets. What does God say about this?

Every Christian is now declared to be a priest. "But ye are a chosen generation, a royal priesthood, an holy nation, a peculiar people; that ye should show forth the praises of him who hath called you out of darkness into his marvelous light" (1 Pet. 2:9). "John to the seven churches which are in Asia: Grace be unto you, and peace, from him which is, and which was, and which is to come; and from the seven Spirits which are before his throne; and from Jesus Christ, who is the faithful witness, and the first begotten of the dead, and the prince of the kings of the earth. Unto him that loved us, and washed us from our sins in his own blood, and hath made us kings and priests unto God and his Father; to him be glory and dominion for ever and ever. Amen" (Rev. 1:4-6).

The death of Christ eliminated the formal Jewish priest-hood. The veil in the Temple which symbolized the separation of mankind from God, was torn "from the top to the bottom" when He died and He became our High Priest and opened direct access to God (Heb. 10:18-21). Now we can enter into the presence of God through His sacrifice. Jesus is our High Priest, our Sacrifice and our Mediator. We need no other.

Everyone who accepts the Sacrificial Lamb of God as his atonement for sin, *everyone* who becomes a Christian is part of this chosen generation and is included in this royal priesthood, including women and Negroes. We have the authority of the Word of God and the indwelling Holy Spirit who has promised to guide us in His truth, the Word of God. We are *all* appointed His ambassadors, which gives us immense and certain author-ity (see 2 Cor. 5:17-21). This is not true of the Mormon "priesthood."

Genealogical records were completely destroyed by the Romans. These genealogical records were kept meticulously by the Jews because of family lines and tribal inheritance. Both Matthew and Luke record the genealogy of Christ. God al-lowed this to be included in His Word so that the Messiahship of Jesus Christ could be proven. Hundreds of years before Jesus Christ, prophets told that He would come from a certain people, from a certain tribe, from a certain family line, from a certain individual within a family. This was part of God's magnificent proof that Jesus Christ was God in the flesh as He claimed to be.

After Jesus was crucified, Titus, in A.D., 70 destroyed all the genealogical records in Jerusalem. All that remained were those recorded in God's Word. God was saying, "The Messiah has come and He has been genealogically verified. It is finished."

Genealogical records were the means of proving the qualifi-cations of priests. Their bloodlines could be traced all the way back to Aaron. When God instituted the Jewish priesthood He chose only one of the 12 tribes of Israel, the Levites, to be priests. Within the tribe of Levi He chose one man, Aaron, as His high priest. All true priests were descendants of Aaron (see Exod. 28:1; 31:10; Lev. 8:2; 9; Num. 3:1-4). Anyone other than a blood descendant of Aaron, who claimed to be a priest, was a false priest, regardless of how many voices they heard or visions they saw claiming that God had given them the authority of the priesthood. Aaronic descent had to be proven.

When God allowed these genealogical records to be totally destroyed, after having miraculously preserved them for centuries, He made it impossible for anyone to trace bloodline descent back to Aaron and thus claim to be an Aaronic priest! Anyone who claims to be an Aaronic priest today is a false priest.

Furthermore, God warns against giving "heed to fables and endless genealogies, which minister questions, rather than godly edifying which is in faith" (1 Tim. 1:4). Again His Word says, "Avoid foolish questions, and genealogies, and contentions, and strivings about the law; for they are unprofitable and vain" (Titus 3:9). The Jewish system is discarded by God in this age of grace. Only those who would out-Hebrew the Hebrews, would cling to a system long set aside by God. This is why we find *no* priests listed—Aaronic, Melchizedek or any other kind—in the church Jesus established! There is no such office today. The New Testament church had no need for them and any church that has an official order of priests is not a New Testament church. It is not a Christian church, whatever else it may be.

The Latter-day Saints make much ado about their Aaronic and Melchizedek priesthood. In the love of Christ we beg them to reconsider. Do not build up what God has torn down. There are not, there cannot be, any priests today. We do not doubt the integrity and sincerity of many who claim to be priests or of those who believe them to be. But to try to restore what God has done away with and put men at least partly back under works instead of wholly under the blood of Christ for full and complete salvation is tragic, both now and eternally, to them and to those who follow them.

Not even Paul or Peter claimed to be priests, except in the sense that every Christian is. As priests, those of us who have accepted the biblical Christ can approach God for ourselves through the blood of the Lord Jesus Christ. We became priests when we obtained His full, free and forever salvation.

Not long ago a dedicated Mormon assured me that he was depending on Jesus alone for his salvation. I said, "Suppose someone not in the Mormon church accepted Christ and depended on Him alone to get him into the 'highest heaven.' Would that person make it?"

The Mormon was suddenly silent, mute evidence that consciously or unconsciously he is depending on Christ plus the Mormon church. According to the Scripture, the only way to salvation is by accepting Jesus Christ as *all-sufficient*, plus nothing (see Eph. 2:8,9).

Consider the parable Jesus told about the Pharisee and the publican in Luke 18:9-14. The Pharisee undeniably belonged to the "one true church" in the sense that he belonged to the worship system God established in the Old Testament. His system still retained priests, men like Caiaphas, and they were still legitimate as this came before the cross. Therefore, the Pharisee could boast that he was in the one true church that God established, and his church contained the one and only authoritative priesthood. He was very religious and, apparently by man's standards, very good. He prayed, "God, I thank thee, that I am not as other men are, extortioners, unjust, adulterers, or even as this publican. I fast twice in the week, I give tithes of all that I possess" (Luke 18:11,12). He was faithful in church, he believed in God, he tithed every cent, he was fair in business and did not get money by force or dishonesty. He treated his neighbor right, paid his debts and was true to his wife.

The publican on the other hand was a mess. He was a Jew who was considered to have sold out to the Roman conquerors. He collected taxes from the Jews for the Romans. One way such despised publicans made their way was by collecting more tax than the Romans levied and pocketing the difference. Some became rich by this means. The publican had *no good works* to commend him to God whatsoever. It is significant that he said nothing to God about prayers, tithe, or not being an adulterer. He was a sinful, hopeless, dishonest wretch. Mormon friends, *which* of these two men would you let into heaven?

The publican prayed, not even lifting his eyes toward heaven, beating on his breast in his agony of need and conviction of sin, "God be *merciful* to me, a sinner."

Which man went home "justified" free from sin, saved? God said, of the publican, "This man went down to his house justified, [saved, forgiven, made right with God] *rather* than the other."

Many Mormon friends say to me with great vehemence, "Do you mean to say that a man who went to church, lived right, paid his debts, etc. could die and miss heaven, and that a man who lied, stole, cheated, and lived a wicked life, could say, 'Jesus save me,' and be saved in the last days or hours of his life? Nonsense!" Yes, that is exactly what I mean to say and the Bible verifies it (see Jesus' encounter with the thief on the cross, Luke 23:39-43; also the parable of the laborers in the vineyard, Matthew 20:1-16). Mormons cannot understand how God's grace can apply to those who have not worked for salvation, who have not earned it.

We all have a sin nature. No amount of works can ever change that, only Jesus can. At whatever point in life you accept Christ as your personal Saviour, it is then that you become a *new creation* in Christ. Then good works will flow from you, not to buy your salvation, but in love and gratitude, proof that you have been saved. The blood of the Lord Jesus

Christ can wash anyone clean whenever he comes honestly, with all his heart to Him. Nothing else will satisfy God.

My good friend, Marvin Cowan, for years a dedicated Mormon and converter of others to Mormonism, told me poignantly how earnestly he believed in and labored for the Mormon church before he met the Lord Jesus Christ and was freed from this system. Now he is a Baptist missionary to Mormons whom he loves and for whom his heart aches. He is another of many who has said hello to Jesus and good-bye to priests. His heart's desire, and mine, is to win Mormons to Jesus Christ. Mormon or non-Mormon, any hungry heart reading this, won't you say hello, once and for all, to Jesus right now?

"Behold, I stand at the door, and knock: if any man hear my voice, and open the door, I will come in to him, and will sup with him, and he with me" (Rev. 3:20).

Footnotes

1. Talmage, *Articles of Faith,* pp. 204–211.

2. B. H. Roberts, *A Comprehensive History of The Church of Jesus Christ of Latter-day Saints* (Salt Lake City: Deseret News Press, 1930), vol. 1, p. 40.

3. Bruce R. McConkie, *Mormon Doctrine* (Salt Lake City: Bookcraft Inc., 1966), p. 477.

4. Joseph Fielding Smith, *Doctrines of Salvation,* vol. 2, p. 149.

5. Wallace Turner, *The Mormon Establishment* (Boston: Houghton Mifflin Co., 1966), pp. 81, 82.

CHAPTER TEN

Some Distinctive but Dubious Doctrines of Mormonism

Some of the most distinctive doctrines of the Mormon church are not found in the *Book of Mormon* but in some of their other sacred writings. In this chapter we will discuss the Mormon's view on plural marriage, hell, baptism for the dead, the three heavens, pre-existence and Negroes.

Polygamy

In the beginning, God provided one wife for Adam. (See Gen. 2:18-25.) Here we again are not dealing with speculation or theory, but with biblical fact.

God instituted marriage with one wife for one man. After sin began to darken the heart of man, he often took more than one wife. More often than not, this was to man's sorrow as well as God's.

Under grace in the New Testament God definitely limited man to one wife. Anything else was adultery. "A bishop then must be blameless, the husband of one wife, vigilant, sober, of good behavior, given to hospitality, apt to teach" (1 Tim. 3:2). God did not and does not have one standard for bishops (pastors) and another for other Christians. This merely means that a bishop had to be a proven, practicing Christian, the husband of only one wife.

The *Book of Mormon* agrees with the Bible on this: "Behold, David and Solomon truly had many wives and concubines, which thing was abominable before me, saith the Lord" (Jacob 2:24). Jacob 3:5 also states that the commandment of the Lord was to have one wife. Yet the prophet Joseph Smith later had a revelation recorded in *Doctrine and Covenants* 132:4. "For behold, I reveal unto you a new and an everlasting [*mark* that word!] covenant; and if ye abide not that covenant, then are ye damned."

Smith then proceeded to elaborate on the doctrine of man being allowed more than one wife. In fact, if a man did not keep this covenant he would be damned. Smith went on to say in *Doctrine and Covenants* 132:38,39 that God had in fact *given* David and Solomon their wives. Finally, Joseph Smith even concludes that the Lord even *justified* his servants David and Solomon in having many wives!

Now Joseph Smith received this convenient revelation on July 12, 1843. He was killed in 1844. Several Mormon writers claim that Smith had as many as 48 wives. Even the most charitable view could hardly avoid the strong implication that Joseph Smith was living in adultery long before he got his "revelation."

It is interesting to notice that included in Joseph Smith's revelation was a warning for his wife, Emma Smith, to receive the other wives. Check the tense also. "Receive all those that *have been given* unto my servant Joseph..." (*Doctrine and Covenants* 132:52).

This doctrine was against the law of the land, and accounted for a great deal of the persecution Mormons received.

Perhaps in an attempt to buoy up the revelation of Joseph Smith, other Mormon leaders went even farther in trying to make this doctrine valid. In speaking of the marriage in Cana, Orson Hyde states that Jesus Christ was married at Cana of Galilee; Mary, Martha and others were His wives.[1] This is ridiculous if not blasphemous. Obviously the eternal Creator, which Jesus is, would not marry a creature. In John 2:2 we are told that Jesus "was called [invited], and his disciples, to the marriage." It is not customary for one to get an invitation to one's own wedding. In John 2:8-10 the *bridegroom* not *Jesus,* is congratulated by the ruler of the feast for the quality of the wine. The ruler of the feast was not aware of the miracle Jesus performed.

Orson Pratt, another Mormon leader, in the *Seer,* page 159, claimed that Jesus had wives.

This polygamous teaching of the Mormons is one more indication that Mormons believe in a Christ who is totally different than the one taught in the Bible. They mean another Christ. Another Jesus or a false Christ, the Bible warns, can never save no matter how sincerely one accepts him. The non-eternal Christ of the Mormons who had to "attain" His way to being God, who was a polygamist, and, as the Mormons also teach, a created being and a brother of the devil, can save no one. The name may be the same, the terms the Mormons use may be similar, but the Person is entirely different.

The Mormons clung tenaciously to the doctrine of polygamy as espoused by their prophet Joseph Smith until the pressure of the law became so great that they had to give up the open practice. President Wilford Woodruff got a convenient "revelation" from God in time to avoid increasing government pressure and prosecution against polygamy. On September 25, 1890, he issued a manifesto declaring the Mormons' intentions of obeying the law of the land to have only one wife. Mormons pledged their honor to keep this law, but many of the Mormon leaders later admitted in public that they had broken the pledge and taken other wives.

The Mormons are in a dilemma. Brigham Young, the Mormon inspired prophet said, "The only men who become Gods, even the Sons of God, are those who enter into polygamy."[2] Joseph Smith had said that those who did not fully accept this doctrine would be damned. The *Book of Mormon* says one wife only, anything else is an abomination to God. President Woodruff said God told him (decide for yourself if by revelation as he claimed or by government pressure) that the everlasting covenant was nullified! Back to one wife!

It seems to us that Mormons are damned if they do and damned if they don't, insofar as plural marriage is concerned. Remember please, God said He is not the author of confusion.

It is rather difficult to understand if Joseph Smith's revelation was *everlasting* how it could be annulled even temporarily. Does this not make the word "everlasting" almost meaningless?

Hell

Jesus Christ taught much about hell. Of the 24 times hell is mentioned in the New Testament, 22 of those times Jesus, the lover of our souls, is the speaker. His description of hades in Luke 16 is very graphic.

Jesus told about a man named Lazarus who died and was "carried into Abraham's bosom." A rich man (Dives in the Greek), in this actual, factual account also died and went to hell. It does not in the least matter whether or not we agree that there is a hell as far as the truth of this account is concerned. Jesus does not lie and He said there is an eternal hell for the lost. The Bible definitely, plainly teaches that there is a hell, and describes the final form of it in Revelation 20:15: "And whosoever was not found written in the book of life was cast into the lake of fire."

The *Book of Mormon* pretty well agrees with the Bible about hell. "And behold, others he [the devil] flattereth away, and telleth them there is no hell; and he saith unto them: I am no devil, for there is none—and thus he whispereth in their ears, until he grasps them with his awful chains, from whence there is no deliverance. Yea, they are grasped with death, and hell; and death, and hell, and the devil, and all that have been seized therewith must stand before the throne of God, and be judged according to their works, from whence they must go into the place prepared for them, even a lake of fire and brimstone, which is endless torment" (2 Nephi 28:22,23).

In spite of these plain declarations in the Bible and the *Book of Mormon,* John A. Widtsoe, a noted Mormon authority and writer and an apostle in the Mormon church, states, "In the Church of Jesus Christ of Latter-day Saints, there is no Hell..."[3]

Other Mormon authorities teach that hell is not eternal; it will have an end—a sort of limited, one-thousand-year or so purgatory for the lost. In trying to research what the Mormons teach on hell we run the gamut from apostles, teachers and inspired books that teach an endless hell, others that teach a limited hell, and still others that teach no hell at all. *As it is on so many other Mormon beliefs, Mormon leaders, their books and their church members are hopelessly divided and do not seem to know what they really believe.*

If you think this is an unfair exaggeration, check the writings of 10 or so Mormon apostles on the subject of hell, read about hell in the three inspired Mormon books, then ask 10 dedicated Mormons what they believe about hell.

Some Mormon leaders, in an attempt to evade the awful horror of hell, try to explain it away by saying that any punishment from God is eternal because God is eternal. Therefore, only one moment of punishment from God would seem like an eternity. Conversely, however, they do not like to consider that one minute's blessing would be the same as an eternal blessing. Would heaven last only one minute? When Jesus said, "These shall go away into everlasting punishment: but the righteous into life eternal" (Matt. 25:46), did He indicate that everlasting life and heaven itself are temporary or fleeting? If God's eternal blessings mean forever, so do His eternal condemnations.

The same Greek word, *aionios,* that is used to describe the eternal continuance of hell is also used to describe the eternal continuance of God and the eternal continuance of heaven! So if God is eternal or everlasting, and if heaven is everlasting, then hell also is everlasting.

Even when the Bible refers to the "second death" (Rev. 2:11; 20:14), in speaking of those who go to hell, it does not mean they cease to exist. Revelation 14:11 and numerous other verses tell us about the eternal anguish and torment of those in hell. When God says that all men are "dead in trespasses and sins" (Eph. 2:1) before they personally come to Christ He does not mean they cease to exist. Even though they feel, think, eat, breathe, etc., God says they are dead. "Dead" in these instances refers not to loss of being, but loss of well-being; it doesn't mean extinction, but ruin.

In the *Book of Mormon* we read: "For behold, if ye have procrastinated the day of your repentance even unto death, behold, ye have become subjected to the spirit of the devil, and he doth seal you his; therefore, the Spirit of the Lord hath withdrawn from you, and hath no place in you, and the devil hath all power over you; and this is the final state of the wicked" (Alma 34:35).

The Bible and the *Book of Mormon* both undeniably teach an eternal hell. When other Mormon apostles and writers deny the existence of an eternal hell, they hopelessly contradict not only the Bible but also the *Book of Mormon.*

Baptism

If the final state of the wicked is sealed with the devil in hell, as the *Book of Mormon* teaches, it seems futile that Mormons would be baptized as substitutes for those who have already died.

Mormons believe that baptism is one of the essentials for salvation. Those who never heard the gospel or were never baptized, or lived and died before the restored gospel, cannot be saved unless someone living is baptized for them. This doctrine was not taught in the *Book of Mormon* but was the result of later revelations of Joseph Smith. Accounts of these are found in *Doctrines and Covenants,* sections 124 and 128.

In all the Bible, covering many centuries, there is not one command that we should be baptized by proxy for the dead. In *Doctrines and Covenants* 128:16, Joseph Smith refers to 1 Corinthians 15:29 to support his doctrine of baptizing for the dead: "Else what shall they do which are baptized for the dead, if the dead rise not at all? Why are they then baptized for the dead?" Here is one example where Mormons take a verse out of context.

The subject of the passage in 1 Corinthians is *resurrection,* not baptism. The whole of 1 Corinthians 15 gives God's beautiful picture of the resurrection of Christ and of our own resurrection if we are Christians. (The resurrection of the ungodly is covered in other references, i.e. Rev. 20.) Paul is answering many questions about the resurrection. He says that even those pagans who baptize for their dead, do so because they believe that there is a resurrection of the dead. "Else what shall *they* do who are baptized for the dead, if the dead rise not at all? Why are *they* then baptized for the dead?" (italics added). His comments do not identify himself or any other Christian with those who baptize for the dead. He is simply acknowledging the fact that even pagans believe in the resurrection of the dead; how much more should Christians.

We know of two pagan groups during Paul's time that baptized for the dead, the Cerinthians (not Corinthians!) and the Marcionites. Christians did not and do not now baptize for the dead. This single reference to baptism for the dead makes no comment of approval or disapproval; it does not say that the dead are helped or saved. Paul used this as an illustration.

The Bible unmistakably teaches that there is no chance whatsoever for men to be saved after death. The fate of the lost is then sealed immediately and forever, once and for all. That is why missionaries of the cross go forth with such urgency in obedience to the command of Christ. That is why they sacrifice and die, that others may hear the gospel. What is the use if, after the lost die, Christ Himself will preach the gospel to them?

As a missionary to Alaska, I faced threats of death; I saw my beautiful little daughter ill with rheumatic fever as we lived in a bitterly cold and uninsulated cabin, without electricity or running water. I suffered the beating of my children and saw my lovely wife fight for her health as we sought to spread the gospel to the lost. Yet ours was a picnic compared to what many godly missionaries endure for a lifetime, not just for a couple of quick years, for Jesus Christ and His precious gospel. These missionaries are willing to bury their lives, their ambitions, and leave their families to risk hardship and death all because they know men are lost without Christ! These lost people have *no hope* if they are not reached while they are *alive*!

There is no chance after death. "Now is the accepted time, now is the day of salvation" (see 2 Cor. 6:2). "As it is appointed unto men once to die, but after this the judgment" (Heb. 9:27). There is no salvation for those who do not believe in Christ, "He that believeth on the Son hath everlasting life: and he that believeth not the Son shall not see life; but the wrath of God abideth on him" (John 3:36).

All men are resurrected: the saved to life everlasting life (see John 6:40) and the unsaved unto damnation (see John 5:29; Rev. 20:3-6). Revelation 20:15 adds the final word on the unsaved: "And whosoever was not found written in the book of life was cast into the lake of fire."

Heaven

In *Doctrine and Covenants* 76, Joseph Smith taught that there are three heavens or three degrees of glory. The first heaven is the *telestial* glory where even unbelievers go. The *terrestrial* or second heaven is for good and religious folks who aren't Mormons, and also those Mormons who have not measured up to all the Mormon requirements for celestial glory. The third heaven is the *celestial* glory which is for Mormons only!

Biblically, Mormons attempt to base this doctrine on 1 Corinthians 15:35-54. Part of this passage reads, "All flesh is not the same flesh: but there is one kind of flesh of men, another flesh of beasts, another of fishes, and another of birds. There are also celestial bodies, and bodies terrestrial: but the glory of the celestial is one, and the glory of the terrestrial is another. There is one glory of the sun, and another glory of the moon, and another glory of the stars: for one star differeth from another star in glory" (1 Cor. 15:39-41).

In this glorious resurrection passage, the subject is definitely bodies, not heaven or heavens per se. In verses 35-38 Paul uses grain as an illustration of the difference in our bodies after the resurrection. He then illustrates his point with a reference to the different flesh of humans, animals, fish and birds (v. 39). Then he refers to the difference in human and possibly angel or celestial bodies (v. 40). Finally, he refers to the different glory of the sun, moon and stars in their individual, personally identifiable kinds of glory (v. 41).

Then in verse 43 Paul says our earthly bodies, which die and decay, are different from our resurrection bodies. Our resurrection bodies are glorified bodies, yet retain their human and their personal identity. Here Paul simply emphasizes the fact that there is a vast difference in the glory of bodies in heaven and bodies on earth. "There is one glory of the sun, and another glory of the moon, and another glory of the stars: for one star differeth from another star in glory" (v. 41). The subject is still resurrection *bodies,* not three different heavens.

Now Paul swings right back into the point of his illustration in verse 42, "So also is the resurrection of the dead. It [the body] is sown in corruption; it is raised in incorruption" (v. 42). The main difference in glory that Paul is talking about is the difference between the body we now have, our natural body, and, if we are Christians, the glorious, resurrection, spiritual body we shall have.

Again, the subject of this passage is *bodies* not heavens. This passage does not teach three heavens as Joseph Smith and the Mormons claim. The context gives no support to such a claim. Indeed, the same context talks about one star differing from another star in glory. To be consistent then, Mormons should teach millions of different heavens or degrees of glory, because there are millions of stars that differ from one another in glory.

Marv Cowan, CBHMS missionary to the Mormons says, "Paul mentions *four* kinds of flesh. Does this verse teach there are four heavens? That reasoning is just as valid as what the LDS do with the next two verses."[4]

The thief on the cross cried out to Jesus and was instantly saved and assured he would be that very day with Christ in paradise. Paul, the mightiest missionary this world has ever seen, a tremendous apostle, and one of the Holy men through whom God gave His Word, was caught up to the third heaven. (According to the Mormons, that is the highest heaven there is.) Guess who was already there? That's right, the thief who was unbaptized, had no good works, temple works or religion whatsoever to recommend him! He was saved by the blood of the Lord Jesus Christ. He was saved instantly and forever because he called believingly on Jesus Christ and had his sins washed away and his nature changed by Jesus. Proof? The third heaven is also called paradise! Read it for yourself! "I knew a man in Christ above fourteen years ago, (whether in the body, I cannot tell; or whether out of the body, I cannot tell:

God knoweth;) such an one caught up to the *third heaven.* And I knew such a man, (whether in the body, or out of the body, I cannot tell: God knoweth;) How that he was caught up into *paradise,* and heard unspeakable words, which it is not lawful for a man to utter" (2 Cor. 12:2-4, italics added). This clearly and totally contradicts what the Mormons teach about heaven and how to get there. Paul goes on in the passage to reveal that it was himself who was caught up into paradise, the third heaven, where Jesus took the saved thief.

In actual fact, there is but *one heaven of God.* Both in Scripture and Hebrew usage, three heavens are spoken of, but the first is the heaven of the clouds, the second is the heaven of the sun, moon and stars, and the third is the *one and only* heaven of God.

The heaven of clouds and atmosphere. "The Lord shall open unto thee his good treasure, the heaven to give the rain unto thy land in his season" (Deut. 28:12). "Who covereth the heaven with clouds, who prepareth rain for the earth" (Ps. 147:8).

The heaven of sun, moon and stars. Genesis 1:17, speaking of the sun and moon, "God set them in the firmament of the heaven to give light upon the earth."

The heaven of God. "Thus saith the Lord, The heaven is my throne" (Isa. 66:1).

There is not one indication in all the Bible that there is more than one heaven of God. On the contrary consider this: "And if I go and prepare *a* place for you, [one only, not three] I will come again, and receive you unto myself; that where I am, there ye may be also!" (John 14:3). Jesus is here speaking to all Christians and assuring them that He will come back for *all* of them and that they will *all be together* with Him (and surely Jesus will be in the "highest heaven," the only heaven of God) in one place forever!

"And then shall he send his angels, and shall *gather together* his elect from the four winds, from the uttermost part of the earth to the uttermost part of heaven" (Mark 13:27).

"For the Lord Himself shall descend from heaven with a shout, with the voice of the archangel, and with the trump of God: and the dead in Christ shall rise first: Then we which are alive and remain shall be caught up together with them in the clouds, to meet the Lord in the air; and so shall we ever be with the Lord" (1 Thess. 4:16, 17).

There is *one heaven,* and *one hell,* and we go to either the one or the other, depending on what we do with Jesus Christ.

Preexistence

Though this is a complicated doctrine from the Mormon standpoint, we want to mention only a few simple facts. Basically, Mormons teach that men were eternally existing intelligences, then men entered the pre-mortal spirit world by birth as God had sexual relations with one of His wives.[5] Oddly enough, this God whom Mormons believe has a body of flesh and bone, had children that are spirits only.

Such verses as Jeremiah 1:5 are called upon by the Mormons in support of the doctrine that we existed as spirits before we were born as humans: "Before I formed thee in the [womb] I knew thee; and before thou camest forth out of the womb I sanctified thee, and I ordained thee a prophet unto the nations."

As is customary, a tremendous superstructure has been built on this exceedingly skimpy and ambiguous foundation.

A Mormon lady, wife of a local Mormon leader, considerably shaken by some of the facts I had been sharing with her, phoned several nights ago concerning this text. "Doesn't this prove we existed before we were born if God knew us before we were formed in the womb?" she asked.

Absolutely not! Not any more than Matthew 7:23, "And then will I profess unto them, I *never knew* you: depart from me, ye that work iniquity" would prove that there were people existing whom God was not aware of!

There are two possibilities. We do not know the exact

moment that life enters a fetus. This reference in Jeremiah could conceivably refer to that time before the fetus was fully developed in the womb and yet had life. The second and most plausible from my viewpoint, is that this is merely speaking of God's foreknowledge. Surely Mormons do not believe that Jeremiah was actually ordained as a prophet in the spirit world before he had a body! Yet if we claim that God literally knew Jeremiah before he was born, to be consistent we also have to literally accept what God said about ordaining him as a prophet before he had a body, while he was yet in the spirit world! Even more of a problem for the Mormons is that this verse not only says that God knew Jeremiah and ordained him as a prophet before he was formed in the womb, but that He also sanctified him. To Mormons, this whole life is a probationary period, but this interpretation would indicate that Jeremiah had it made before he was even born!

Now look closely at Acts 15:18: "Known unto God are all his works from the beginning of the world." This speaks of God's foreknowledge of all things. It most certainly does not mean that His works existed before He made them! If God knew His works from the beginning of the world, that certainly includes the earth. It does not mean that the earth existed before He made it! Jeremiah is one of God's works. It certainly does not mean that Jeremiah existed before he was born. God's works included the creation of Adam. It emphatically does not mean that Adam existed before he was created any more than it means that the earth existed before it was created. Romans 8:28-30 gives highlights of God's wonderful foreknowledge, without which He would not be God, and all of our security for eternity would be gone.

God said in Genesis 2:7, "And the Lord God formed man out of the dust of the ground, and breathed into his nostrils the breath of life; and man became a living soul." That is when man's life started. He had no life before, anywhere at any time. Notice that God did not put into Adam one of His pre-existent spirit children which only exist in Mormon literature. Man got life for the first time direct from God.

The Negro

According to Mormon doctrine, because of some supposed pre-existent sin (i.e., not being as "valiant" in fighting for God's side against Satan and His angels as some others were), the Negro was cursed with a black skin. This curse was perpetuated through Ham. Because of this, the black is *forever* (according to Mormon books and authorities) forbidden the priesthood, the highest heaven, etc. It would not be too surprising, if present day pressure continues to mount against this unpopular and unsupportable doctrine, to hear of a new "revelation" from LDS headquarters. This revelation would contradict or soften the former God-given, forever forbidden doctrine. This would not be unique in LDS history.

Mormon writer, Arthur M. Richardson, declares, "The Church of Jesus Christ of Latter-day Saints has no call to carry the gospel to the Negro, and it does not do so."[6]

Richardson's view clearly contradicts Mark 16:15: "Go ye into all the world, and preach the gospel to every creature" (black, red, white or whatever).

It also contradicts the *Book of Mormon,* 2 Nephi 26:28: "Behold, hath the Lord commanded any that they should not partake of his goodness? Behold, I say unto you, Nay; but *all* men are privileged the one like unto the other, and none are forbidden" (italics added).

Could a revelation from God exclude millions of precious souls for whom Christ also died? Millions of blacks would go to hell forever with no hope if their salvation were left up to Mormonism. At best, they are religious peons, doomed to be second class both here and hereafter, according to Mormon theology. They are tolerated in the Mormon church, but never sought with the burning love of Christ for the lost. Many a precious African and American black can thank God this

LDS movement came late and is relatively small. If this were Christianity, *No Hope* would be the black man's eternal epitaph.

Footnotes

1. Orson Hyde, *Journal of Discourses,* vol. 2, p. 210.

2. Brigham Young, *Journal of Discourses,* vol. 11, p. 269. (See also vol. 3, p. 266.)

3. John A. Widtsoe, *Evidences and Reconciliation* (Salt Lake City: Bookcraft, 1960), p. 216.

4. Marvin W. Cowan, *Mormon Claims Answered,* p. 101.

5. Milton R. Hunter, *Gospel Through the Ages* (Salt Lake City: Deseret Books, 1945), pp. 98, 126–129.

6. Arthur M. Richardson, *That Ye May Not Be Deceived,* p. 13. Quoted by Tanner, *Mormonism, Shadow or Reality,* p. 274.

CHAPTER ELEVEN

The One True Church

There is a very curious thing about the claims of Mormonism. At one time they can convey the idea that they are a legitimate Christian body, whose doctrines, except in a few particulars, are not very different from the usual Christian statement of faith. Yet, at the same time they subscribe to a church whose inspired books proclaim that all other churches are wrong, all their creeds are an abomination, and all their professors are corrupt!

Concerning the Mormon creed, the "Articles of Faith" which can be found in the *Pearl of Great Price,* it is confusing to consider why *all other creeds* are an abomination to God, but when the tenets of these creeds are transferred verbatim to the Mormon "creed" they suddenly become holy and acceptable to God!

If all our creeds are an abomination, as Joseph Smith proclaimed by revelation, "all their creeds were an abomination in his sight" (Joseph Smith 2:19, *Pearl of Great Price*), we would hardly expect the Mormon "Articles of Faith" to adapt the fundamental beliefs contained in them as their own.

More confusing still is the inspired teaching by Smith in the *Book of Mormon* and by divinely guided Mormon apostles who declare, "All will be damned who are not Latter-day Saints." [1] Again, we read, "Both Catholics and Protestants are nothing less than the 'whore of Babylon' whom the Lord denounces by the mouth of John the Revelator as having corrupted all the earth by their fornications and wickedness. Any person who shall be so wicked as to receive a holy ordinance of the Gospel from the ministers of any of these apostate churches will be sent down to hell with them, unless they repent of the unholy and impious act." [2] (Yet in other Mormon books we are told that we will be in one of the two lowest heavens or degrees of glory.)

The Mormons claim to be the one true church in a number of their books, but we will quote *Doctrine and Covenants* 1:30. Here the Mormon church is called, "the only true and living church upon the face of the whole earth."

What the Mormon church really teaches is, "There is no salvation outside... the Church [of Jesus Christ of Latter-day Saints]." [3]

In the *Book of Mormon,* 1 Nephi 13:26, Joseph Smith wrote, "A great and abominable church... [has] taken away from the gospel of the Lamb many parts which are plain and most precious; and also many covenants of the Lord have they taken away." This reference is to the churches that supposedly apostatized. Now the *Book of Mormon* dates this writing around 600 B.C., six hundred years *before* Christ came, before there was any gospel of the Lamb, and certainly before there were any Christian churches to which Smith refers.

This is one of the reasons, nevertheless, that Smith uses to show the need for the *Book of Mormon* and the one true church. *All* other churches became false, and all the Christians were corrupt and the true gospel disappeared from off the earth. The gospel had to be "restored" and a new revelation given.

Jesus said explicitly, in Matthew 24:35, "Heaven and earth shall pass away, but my words shall not pass away!"

Again, Jesus declared in Matthew 28:20 that He would be with His church and His people "Alway, *even* to the end of the world." *Alway. Continuously.* Just who was Jesus going to be with if there were not any church or Christians left on earth a short while after He died? And Jesus further claimed, in Matthew 16:18, "I will build my church; and the gates of hell shall not prevail against it."

If Mormonism is true, what Jesus said was untrue. For Mormons say the gates of hell *did* prevail against His church and total apostasy eliminated His true church, His true people, and His true Word off the earth for over a thousand years, to be "restored" by Prophet Smith!

This Mormon doctrine is not only untrue to the Bible, it is utterly untrue to church history. Thousands, indeed even millions scattered around the world, were living for Jesus Christ even during the dark ages. The formal Catholic Church did get far away from God, but Luther and many others were saved even in its corrupt embrace. *Foxe's Book of Martyrs* tells how hundreds of thousands died for Jesus Christ, were burned at the stake, tortured unspeakably, torn apart by wild beasts, all the while proclaiming their undying love for Jesus Christ.

Many other books of church history record how, during these hundreds of years Joseph Smith would have us believe no true believers and no true church was on the earth, Christians died rejoicing in their salvation and praising their wonderful Saviour.

One striking example from among thousands that can be given, were the martyrs of the Theban Legion. A group of Roman soldiers numbering 6,666 men who had accepted

Christ, the Theban Legion, in A.D., 286 refused to deny Christ and make pagan sacrifices. They were cut to pieces with the sword.

There were various Christian groups meeting down through the centuries, long before the Protestant Reformation, who never were a part of the "Mother" church. *Trail of Blood* and many other books of history have preserved the names of these churches for us: Paulicans, Brethren of the Common Lot, Montanist, Paterins, Novations, Arnoldist, Cathari, Albigenses, Waldenses, Henricans, Anabaptists, Baptists, and the well-known names of those churches springing out of the Protestant Reformation such as Lutheran, Presbyterian, Congregational, Methodist, etc.

In 1536, after years of faithfully serving the Lord Jesus Christ and translating the Bible into the language of the people, William Tyndale was burned at the stake, near Antwerp, England, praying until his last breath for those who tortured him. In about 1441, John Huss, a precious, faithful Christian was burned at the stake because of his love and faithfulness to Jesus Christ, and actually sang praises to Jesus until the crackling of the flames drowned out his voice. Please remember, this and thousands of like events happened during the centuries when Joseph Smith says God's true church and true gospel, and His true people had vanished from the earth (later to be restored in 1830 by Prophet Smith!). Millions died for their faith in faithfulness to Jesus Christ during this period of over a thousand years when Joseph Smith claimed that all true Christians, the true church and the true gospel had disappeared from the earth.

According to Joseph Smith and Mormon teaching, no one during this time and no one today is in the one true church except a relatively small group of people called Mormons. Mormons must either believe this teaching, which is contrary to the Bible and church history, or deny the Prophet Joseph Smith.

Some Mormon parents sacrifice a great deal to send their sons out as missionaries. So do these fine, but misled, young men who give two years of their lives to the Mormon cause. According to the August, 1961 *Mormon Missionary Handbook,* Mormon missionaries must lead potential converts to say about their own churches and all other churches, "They are false." In the new, modified and somewhat more subtle and sophisticated *Mormon Missionary Handbook,* this terminology was softened. No change, however, was made in the *Book of Mormon* or in Mormon doctrine, that all other churches are false.

Apostles in the Mormon Church

One of the reasons Mormons give to show that their church is the one true church is that they have "apostles" in their church. These apostles are called the Twelve, and it is believed that they hold the restored office of the original apostles. An ordained apostle is "one who is ordained to the office of apostle in the Melchizedek Priesthood.... This apostleship carries the responsibility of proclaiming the gospel in all the world and also of administering the affairs of the Church. ... The original Twelve in latter-days were selected by revelation to the Three Witnesses to the *Book of Mormon.*"[4]

There are several problems with this claim. In the first place, if we use "apostle" in the narrow sense of an office or as a gift given to certain men chosen of God, the LDS church has too many apostles. Revelation 21:14 says that the wall of God's heavenly "city had twelve foundations, and in them the names of the twelve apostles of the Lamb." The Twelve were personally called by Christ. They were among those who witnessed the living Jesus in His ministry, death and resurrection. As a special sign of their apostleship they worked miracles. (See Matt. 10:7,8; Acts 3:6-8; 5:12-16; 9:37-40; 2 Cor. 12:12.)

The LDS church, up to now, has appointed 80 apostles. Today they have 12 apostles plus three men in the First Presidency who are also apostles. It is true that others were called apostles in the Bible, but only 12 form the *historical foundation* of the church (Rev. 21:14); Christ is now and forever the *theological foundation* of the church (1 Cor. 3:11).

In the second place, if we use "apostle" in the wider sense, the word means "one sent forth" or "sent one." This applies to every Christian who is a true child of God. We are all sent ones, sent out to share Christ. This wider use of apostle was used of Barnabas, Andronicus, Epaphroditus, Junia, etc.

Paul says he was "called to be an apostle, separated unto the gospel of God" (Rom. 1:1). He did not accompany Jesus but was specially and dramatically chosen by God. (See Acts 22:12-15 for an account of Paul's calling; see also 1 Cor. 9:1.) Other apostles founded many of the early churches.

If the title of "apostle" were meant to be a perpetual office in the church, God surely would have left us with a definite list of qualifications, directions as to their duties, authority, purpose and responsibilities. He gave us such directions and qualifications for the offices of bishop (1 Tim. 3:1-7), deacon (1 Tim. 3:8-13), and elder (1 Tim. 5:1-21), but none is given for apostle.

There is still another problem with the Mormon claim that theirs is the only true church because it is founded on the apostles. The Mormon church began in 1830, and the "foundation," the Twelve Apostles, were not chosen until February 14, 1835. What was the status of the Mormon organization during the years before the Twelve Apostles?

The New Testament speaks of "false apostles," "I know thy works, and thy labour, and thy patience, and how thou canst not bear them which are evil: and thou hast tried them which say they are apostles, and are not, and hast found them liars" (Rev. 2:2).

Prophets in the Mormon Church

In a previous chapter we discussed the role of prophets as

114

foretellers of the future, under the guidance of God. We discussed the test for a prophet as given in the Scriptures. We cited many cases where Joseph Smith did not meet the prophet test, neither have any of his successors which proves beyond doubt that they were false prophets.

Prophets of God, though undoubtedly students of the Scriptures, did not get their message by study but by direct revelation from God. True prophets, those who foretold future events under God's guidance with 100 percent accuracy all the time, and those who received direct revelations foretelling the future, have passed away.

Now that we have the completed Word of God, the foretelling of future events is unnecessary. God's written Word is sufficient. Since the New Testament prophets passed from the scene no so-called prophet, in this sense, has passed the prophet-test. All are false prophets.

Unfortunately, this often did not deter their followers who failed to heed or apply God's test for a true prophet. So, a multitude of cults have been founded by so-called prophets of God that delude precious men and women and lead to a lost eternity.

Hebrews 1:1,2 aptly sums it up for us: "God, who at sundry times and in divers manners spake in time past unto the fathers by the prophets, hath in these last days spoken unto us by his Son, whom he hath appointed heir of all things, by whom also he made the worlds."

Another biblical meaning of the title "prophet" has to do with "forth-telling" of God's Word. Many good men from many different churches still do that when they preach and teach the Word of God.

The One True Church

There is only one "true church" mentioned in the Bible and every true believer—Baptist, Methodist, Lutheran, Presbyterian, whatever—belongs to that Church the moment he re-

115

ceives Christ. There are those who are members of the one true Church who never belonged to any denominational church, the thief on the cross for example! He too now belongs to the one true Church!

First Corinthians 12:13 says that *all* Christians are baptized by the Holy Spirit into the body of Christ. (This is not speaking of water baptism. The Spirit does not baptize us in water.) Ephesians 5:29-32 and other passages tell us that Christ's body in this sense is His Church, and His Church is His body! First Corinthians 12:13, "For by one Spirit are we all baptized into one body, whether we be Jews or Gentiles, whether we be bond or free; and have been all made to drink into one Spirit."

So every Christian is in the one true Church, placed there by the Holy Spirit the moment he is saved! We might add that this unity among true Christians does not extend to groups that doubt portions of the Word of God, substitute ritual for reality and social change for the new birth. These have a form of godliness, but deny the power thereof (see 2 Tim. 3:5), and are nominal Christians or Christians in name only.

Being in a good local church is vitally important. Hebrews 10:25 cautions us not to forsake the "assembling of ourselves together." There are hundreds of churches and denominations, and some with no denomination, that teach basically the same thing about Jesus Christ and His wonderful salvation, and also all major, fundamental doctrines of the Bible. That is why hundreds of different churches and denominations can get together happily to hold city-wide evangelistic meetings, or to reach an area for Jesus Christ. Actually, we have far fewer differences on the whole among true Christians of different denominations than Mormons have among themselves. We have a spiritual unity in Christ far greater than any artificial unity of a physical nature.

We do have some differences that are important to us individually. We have different ways of governing our churches where the Bible does not spell out clearly and specifically how it should be done; differences in approach, outreach and doctrines of less than a fundamental nature. Serious Christians seek a church that presents Christ most clearly to them and makes His salvation clear, reaches the lost, stresses that only the blood of Jesus Christ can cleanse us from our sins, and a church that sticks as close to the Word of God as it possibly can.

In Summary

How did the Mormons get so far afield from the truth of the Word of God, so far that "inspired" Prophet Brigham Young could say, "No man or woman in this dispensation will ever enter the celestial Kingdom of God without the consent of Joseph Smith!"[5] This is a direct challenge to the Word of God and to the Lord Jesus Christ, "For there is one God, and one mediator between God and men, the man Christ Jesus" (1 Tim. 2:5). "Neither is there salvation in any other: for there is none other name under heaven given among men, whereby we must be saved" (Acts 4:12). *This name is Jesus.*

Joseph Smith is the man who led the Mormons astray, and still does because they refuse to consider or accept the clear evidence from God in Deuteronomy 18:20-22, and other passages, that he was a false prophet.

Mormons would do well, every time some unfavorable report of Joseph Smith appears, not to shove it under the rug and proclaim that it is the work of anti-Mormons, but to systematically and carefully examine it for truth. Real truth can stand investigation and examination. It is not necessary to look at anti-Mormon sources to find out about the real Joseph Smith. Historical Mormon sources reveal an entirely different Joseph Smith than most Mormons have been shown. Mormons should insist that such publications, which are often withheld in sacred archives even from the Mormon public, should be opened at least to all Mormons.

At times some of this material has been made available and

then withdrawn. We have done our best to be fair and honest with the truths we have discovered. We have ignored or passed over much extremely damaging information, *mostly from Mormon sources,* concerning Joseph Smith's morals, business ethics, truthfulness, treasure-hunting background, etc. We ask Mormons to investigate this honestly and thoroughly for themselves.

Truly, our Mormon friends need to heed Galatians 1:8, and indeed, we all do! "But though we, or an angel from heaven, preach any other gospel unto you than that which we have preached unto you, let him be accursed!"

Footnotes

1. Ora Pate Stewart, *We Believe.* Taken from Keith L. Brook, comp., *The Spirit of Truth and the Spirit of Error* (Chicago, Moody Press, 1963), p. 7.

2. Orson Pratt, *The Seer,* a publication founded by Orson Pratt in memory of the Prophet Joseph Smith, Jr., 1852, p. 255.

3. Bruce R. McConkie, *Mormon Doctrine* (Salt Lake City: Bookcraft, Inc., 1966), p. 138, see also pp. 81, 136).

4. McConkie, *Mormon Doctrine,* p. 47.

5. Brigham Young, *Journal of Discourses,* vol. 7, p. 289.

CHAPTER TWELVE

The Final Authority

When God's people were enticed to consult the mediums and wizards who could perform wonders in the name of God, they were told, "To the law and to the testimony: if they speak not according to *this word*, it is because there is no light in them" (Isa. 8:20, italics added).

The law and the testimony obviously referred to the Word of God. The Bible is God's unchanging plumb-line. Nothing else is!

Consider this: "All scripture is given by inspiration of God, and is profitable for doctrine, for reproof, for correction, for instruction in righteousness" (2 Tim. 3:16). "For the prophecy came not in old time by the will of man: but holy men of God spake as they were moved by the Holy Ghost" (2 Pet. 1:21).

These and many other Scriptures tell us that the Bible is the very Word of God. Fulfilled prophecy, historical and ar-cheological accuracy, unity and harmony beyond compare in a book with some 40 authors and written over a period of some 1500 years, lack of scientific errors common in other ancient books, the life and resurrection of Jesus, and its life-trans-forming power all combine to reinforce this claim.

This same God who gave the Word is well able to preserve it. He has promised to do just that; He has done it and He will continue to do it. God does not lie. "Heaven and earth shall pass away, but my words shall not pass away" (Matt. 24:35). To cast doubt on the Word of God is to take the side of atheists, unbelievers, skeptics and cultists down through the ages. It is to take sides against Christ and true Christians.

Jesus told us to search the Scriptures, in John 5:39, even to proving His claims: "Search the scriptures;...and they are they which testify of me." When Paul and Silas went to Berea with the claims of Christ and of the gospel, the Bereans were praised because they "searched the scriptures daily, whether those things [that Paul and Silas were teaching] were so" (Acts 17:11). The Bereans were using the Old Testament which had been given hundreds of years before and had been translated from the Hebrew into the Greek in a translation called the Septuagint. They did not quibble about the Bible being "the Word of God as far as it is translated correctly."[1]

How different from the Mormon way of finding truth!

The Mormon Test for Authority

Mormons are taught to test the truth of the *Book of Mormon* in their minds, feelings and experience, and also by prayer: "And when ye shall receive these things, I would exhort you that ye would ask God, the Eternal Father, in the name of Christ, if these things are not true; and if ye shall ask with a sincere heart, with real intent, having faith in Christ, he will manifest the truth of it unto you, by the power of the Holy Ghost" (Moroni 10:4, *Book of Mormon*).

The Mormons sometimes declare that they had a "burning bosom," such as is mentioned in *Doctrine and Covenants*: "But, behold, I say unto you, that you must study it out in your mind, then you must ask me if it be right, and if it is right I will cause that your bosom shall burn within you; therefore, you shall feel that it is right" (*Doctrine and Covenants* 9:8). This burning bosom "proved" the Holy Spirit was testifying to them of the truth of the *Book of Mormon* and Mormonism. Thus mind, experience and feeling are substituted for the Bible, and all in the name of God! The Bereans did not depend on a burning bosom from the Holy Spirit; they searched the Scriptures.

Reading the *Book of Mormon* and letting the Holy Spirit testify of its truthfulness to oneself is not God's approved way. *First,* this substitutes another test, another way, for God's way of determining truth or error.

Second, for the most part, Mormon doctrine is not even in the *Book of Mormon.* Though Mormons claim the *Book of Mormon* is the fullness of the everlasting gospel, it does not contain any of the following doctrines which form the heart of Mormonism: 1) Pre-existence, 2) Genealogies, 3) Baptism for the dead, 4) Celestial marriage, 5) Three degrees of glory, 6) Godhood promised to man, 7) Temporary hell, 8) Eternal progression. How can prayer and feeling or experience determine the truth of something that isn't even included in the book you are reading? The Holy Spirit does not lend Himself to such nonsensical "tests!"

Third, and most dangerous, the Holy Spirit is not the only powerful spirit in this world. You might be deceived by trusting only in prayer and feeling or experience. The mighty evil spirit the Bible calls Satan is posing as an "angel of light," and deceiving all he can to an eternal hell. When we set aside God's prescribed way of finding truth, we are totally without protection and open to Satan's delusions.

Someone well asked, "Could a false church appear righteous?" The one who asked this question, a converted Mormon lady, added; "What would be the purpose of a wrong church if not to deceive? If someone were going to make counterfeit money, would they use red ink?"[2]

Notice Satan's program: "For such are false apostles, deceitful workers, transforming themselves into the apostles of Christ. And no marvel: for Satan himself is transformed into an angel of light. Therefore it is no great thing if his ministers also be transformed as the ministers of righteousness; whose end shall be according to their works" (2 Cor. 11:13-15).

Allen Beechick and Bruce Walters, two fine Christian men in our church, recently had a confrontation with several Mormon missionaries. The conversation went something like this:

Allen: "How do you know that the *Book of Mormon* is the Word of God?"

Mormon: "I have prayed about it and I have a *testimony* that I know that it is true and that Joseph Smith, to whom it was given, is a prophet of God."

Allen: "What is your *evidence* that the *Book of Mormon* is true and that Joseph Smith is a prophet of God? How do you 'know' it to be true, in either case?"

Mormon: "I know it is true because I have prayed about it and *feel* that it is true. I also know that it is true because the Mormon church has a living prophet to guide us into all truth."

Allen: "How do you know that this living prophet is a prophet of God?"

Mormon: "I have a *testimony* that our living prophet is a prophet of God."

Allen: "Can Satan give good feelings to deceive? What happens when your feelings say one thing and the Word of God says another? Which is more reliable and which do you believe? I have good feelings about receiving Jesus Christ by faith alone and being saved instantly and being sure of heaven,

122

and this good feeling has already lasted 20 years. Why should your 'good feelings' be any more conclusive than mine? Don't you think the Bible is a much more reliable standard than my 'feelings' or 'testimony' or your 'feelings' or 'testimony?' "

We ask again, can a testimony make a false prophet true or make sense out of obvious nonsense? What can a testimony do to make this prophecy come true: Mormon president Heber C. Kimball prophesied that Brigham Young would become president of the United States.[3] What can a testimony do to nullify this statement: Polygamy will *never* be done away with.[4]

What can a testimony do to verify these revelations given in sermons by Brigham Young that he declared were Scripture: "Gold and silver grow, and so does every other kind of metal, the same as the hair upon my head, or the wheat in the field."[5] Young also taught that the sun as well as the moon were inhabited. Read it for yourself in *Journal of Discourses,* volume 13, page 271.

No amount of "testimony" can ever cover up the fact that these are false prophecies by Mormon prophets. We cannot help but believe that hundreds of thousands of honest Mormons want and deserve better than this. We believe that they can see that the "testimony" has been developed and used as a weapon to keep them in unquestioning ignorance and darkness. Brilliant doctors, lawyers and professors among the Mormons, who would never accept shoddy, unproven and dangerous theories but demand impeccable evidence in their professions, are locked into this system which forces them to accept "facts" like these by their "testimony." In this way they have confused faith with believing what they know is not true.

Biblical faith permits and demands objective, evidential reality, as well as subjective experience. Anything less fosters delusion and dishonesty.

Millions of Christians can testify to a tremendous "testimony" of certainty that the Bible is the *only Word of God,* that they have been saved instantly when they trusted Jesus, and that they are now sure of heaven forever with Jesus Christ. They have peace, joy and transformed lives since their conversion. However, any such testimony must be in full accord with the Bible and its truth or it is false. Feelings can be and have been manipulated. God would not leave our eternal destiny to be decided ultimately by "feelings" or "testimony" of fallible human beings. This is why He furnished so much tremendous evidence in the Bible that it is indeed the Word of God. This is why all claims of truth must be measured by the Bible. God will not bypass this, His final authority.

Authority of the Prophets

Prophets, in the sense of foretelling the future and getting their message directly from God, have fulfilled their role and been set aside in favor of the Son and His completed Word, the Bible: "God, who at sundry times and in divers manners spake in times past unto the fathers by the prophets, hath in these last days spoken unto us by his Son" (Heb. 1:1,2).

This is obvious for at least two reasons. *First,* any "gospel" given directly from God would have to be the same as the gospel of the Word of God *already fully given*; therefore, it would be unnecessary.

Paul declared, "I have fully preached the gospel of Christ" (Rom. 15:19). Not one thing needed to be added to the gospel. (See also Gal. 1:8,9.)

Second, the book of Revelation reveals the church age, the tribulation, millennium and the consummation of all things into the eternal state. All time is covered. God has not forgotten anything so that He would have to add a divine PS by further revelation to a prophet.

Remember, the Old Testament foretold the coming of the Messiah, the Christ. The New Testament tells of the fulfillment of the Old—Christ has come. Hebrews chapters 7 and 8 speak of replacing the Old Covenant with the New Covenant. In Hebrews 13:20 this New Covenant is referred to as an "everlasting covenant." There is no mention in Scripture of a third, or "newer," covenant that might involve further revelation.

Jude 1:3 speaks of the "faith *once for all* delivered to the saints" (literal translation). There is no gospel left to give. There is no revelation left to give. It has already been fully given!

Since no other revelation is needed, prophets, in the sense of getting revelations directly from God and foretelling future events and recording them as God-given Scripture, are no longer in the church today. *All* such so-called prophets today are false.

The Mormons claim that Joseph Smith was a prophet. Read what the Scriptures say about those who preach any other gospel than what God has already given to us: "Many will say to me in that day, Lord, Lord, have we not prophesied in thy name? and in thy name have cast out devils? and in thy name done many wonderful works? And then will I profess unto them, I never knew you: depart from me, ye that work iniquity" (Matt. 7:22,23). "But though we, or an angel from heaven, preach any other gospel unto you than that which we have preached unto you, let him be accursed. As we said before, so say I now again, If any man preach any other gospel unto you than that ye have received, let him be accursed" (Gal. 1:8,9).

What then, is the final authority? The Bible, the Word of God! God has given it. God has preserved it. Any other work that does not square with the gospel already given, is not of God.

The Authority of the "Inspired Bible"

If Joseph Smith truly were a prophet of God, one of the first things God would have him do would be to correct any errors in His Word, the Bible! Surely this makes sense.

As a matter of fact, when Joseph Smith began to have some

problems in coinciding what the *Book of Mormon* taught and what the Bible said, he received a "revelation" to translate the Bible and free it from all "error." God, he said, commissioned him to do this and gave him divine revelation in doing it. This Bible is called the *Inspired Version of the Bible*.[6]

Now immediately the question comes to mind, "If Joseph Smith translated the Bible into an accurate translation, why does the Mormon Article of Faith say, 'We believe the Bible to be the word of God as far as it is translated correctly?' " The *Inspired Version of the Bible* can be purchased in the Deseret Book Store in Salt Lake City, a Mormon-owned business. Yet few Mormons (and exceedingly few non-Mormons!) even know the book exists. Why don't the Mormons joyously bring out this perfect, without error, inspired Bible? Could it be that they cannot trust the *Inspired Version of the Bible* of Joseph Smith? If so, they condemn their prophet as a false prophet, even though he said he got the Bible directly from God, just as he did the *Book of Mormon*.

Perhaps the answer is that they know what the reaction would be if it were shown that Joseph Smith's *Inspired Version of the Bible* still contains virtually word-for-word, about 85 to 90 percent of the King James Bible. This might be embarrassing to the Mormons.

Even more embarrassing perhaps, would be the 17 verses Joseph Smith added to Genesis 50, in which he prophesied and says that he will bring salvation to his people: "And that seer will I bless... and his name shall be called Joseph, and it shall be after the name of his father... for the thing which the Lord shall bring forth by his hand shall bring my people unto salvation" (Gen. 50:33, *Inspired Version of the Bible*).

Jesus often referred to the Scriptures. It seems odd that He would have overlooked something as tremendously important as this passage. Odd too, that Revelation, which deals explicitly with latter days, never mentions Joseph Smith and the prophecy in Genesis!

In Summary

In the love of Christ, I counsel you, Mormon or non-Mormon, to recognize that the Bible is reliable and the only final authority; that departure from it as the standard of truth brings chaos and confusion.

Suppose Satan inspired a book to either supplant or deny the Bible. If the book were judged by the Bible, Satan would be easily found out and thwarted. But if he declared the book he had written to be the Word of God, used some of the real Word of God in it, and used similar wording, the plot would thicken. Then suppose he suggested as proof, that we pray, and ask the Holy Spirit to show us if it was the Word of God or not, and if we were really *sincere* we would know the truth. And, in some cases at least, it might even be confirmed by a "burning in the bosom."

Obviously, Satan could cause us to do a flip-flop. We are no longer judging the book by the known Word of God, the Bible, as we are commanded to do. We are judging the book by feeling, and experience, and asking God to give us proof that something He has already clearly declared false is true! If our burning desire to know the truth and the psychology and emotion of calling on God and desperately seeking an answer doesn't produce some kind of feeling it would be strange indeed!

Could not Satan cause a "feeling" or a "burning in the bosom" to *prove* that the book he inspired was the Word of God? Of course he could. And he does!

Once Satan removes the Bible as a test or final authority, the foundation God gave for judging prophets, religious movements, etc., is lost! Then the person or cult claiming to have a vision, a revelation, a "burning in their bosom that God gave them," has an open field! In this way scores of religious movements and cults have been started.

As soon as we begin to put feelings, experiences, our own intellect, scientific speculations, new prophets or other

127

Scriptures on a par with, and even above the Bible, we lose our foundation and completely reverse the situation. We then begin to judge the Bible by false criteria rather than testing the criteria by the Bible. Immediately, we become disobedient to God and doubt His truth. He can no longer answer our prayers for light and truth because He will not bless disobedience and sin! Even if God were to answer our prayer for discernment under these conditions, "the natural man receiveth not the things of the Spirit of God: for they are foolishness unto him" (1 Cor. 2:14).

I believe that the only reason I was delivered from becoming a Mormon is because I finally searched the Bible. The Holy Spirit opened my eyes to Jesus. My prayers were answered and I had sweet and precious feelings, *but the Bible was the catalyst*. The Bible made it happen! The Bible, not my feelings, was my authority!

When we trust in anything other than the Bible as the authority, we open the door to Satan's delusion that he is an angel of light and minister of righteousness. Satan not only deceives people into hell by making them "bad" people who lust for the things of the world, he also lures many into hell by making them "good" people. Just look at Romans 10:2,3: "For I bear them record that they have a zeal of God, but not according to knowledge. For they being ignorant of God's righteousness, and going about to establish their own righteousness, have not submitted themselves unto the righteousness of God."

This seems to be as perfect a description of the Mormons as it was of the religious but lost Jews of Paul's day. In Luke 16:31, when the rich man in hell pleaded for someone to go from the dead and convince his brothers and save them from hell fire, God's Word declares, "If they hear not Moses and the prophets [the written Word of God], neither will they be persuaded, though one rose from the dead."

It is so difficult to be kind and yet speak the truth. We do not want to sacrifice truth on the altar of kindness, nor sacrifice

128

kindness on the altar of truth. We have earnestly endeavored, by the grace of God, to keep the proper balance and "speak the truth in love." We know the cutting away of malignant tissue involves pain, however good the intentions of the surgeon, even with the use of the best anesthetic. But the results can be life, joy, and health.

Spiritual surgery is often painful also. The intentions may be good but the keen edge of the knife of truth may still cause some pain. The results, however can be eternal life, spiritual health, and great joy! God grant that it may be so to many of our readers!

Several weeks ago, I was presenting Christ and His free and instant salvation to two Mormon ladies. They were leaders in the library and visual aids department of their LDS church. Both ladies asked Jesus to save them. One lady, who has four Mormon sons who served as missionaries, raised her head and exclaimed, "Vivian, Vivian, you know that burning feeling our leaders talk about and you never get, and you wonder what it is? I've got it, I've got it!" Needless to say, she based her instant salvation on Jesus and His word, but felt that this was a bonus. Christians do not ordinarily get or depend on such. God gave this dear lady a special bonus. True Christians do get a deep and abiding peace beyond anything else they have ever known.

Footnotes

1. Articles of Faith #8.
2. Janet Webster, in an open letter to Mormon Friends. Used by permission.
3. Young, *Journal of Discourses,* vol. 5, p. 219.
4. Young, *Journal of Discourses,* vol. 3, p. 125.
5. Young, *Journal of Discourses,* vol. 1, p. 219.
6. Both Joseph Smith and Andrew Jensen in his LDS *Church Chronology* claim the *Inspired Version of the Bible* was completed July 2, 1833. So also claims *Documentary History of the Church,* volume 1, pp. 324, 369; *Times and Seasons,* vol. 6, p. 802.

CHAPTER THIRTEEN

Mormon Salvation

When we speak of obtaining salvation most people recognize one of two ways whereby we think we might be saved: God's way, by free unmerited grace; man's way, by works. The Mormons teach that the way of salvation is by works.

Mormons divide salvation into two parts: 1) unconditional or general salvation, 2) conditional or individual salvation, (sometimes called personal salvation or exaltation).

General Salvation

Mormon theology claims that the death of Christ on the cross ransomed men from the effects of the fall (see McConkie, *Mormon Doctrine,* p. 62; also 669, 670) except for the incorrigible "sons of perdition" (those who fell with Lucifer). All mankind will eventually receive "general salvation," which will get everyone at least into the lowest of the three heavens or degrees of glory.

Stephen L. Richards, in his pamphlet, *Contributions of Joseph Smith,* claims that this salvation is equated with resurrection, for all men will be resurrected—atheists, pagans, unbelievers, etc.[1] It is difficult to fit this belief into John 3:18: "He that believeth on him is not condemned: but he that believeth not is condemned already, because he hath not believed in the name of the only begotten Son of God."

John 3:36 tells us that there is no salvation of any kind for those who do not believe, only condemnation: "He that believeth on the Son hath everlasting life: and he that believeth not the Son shall not see life; but the wrath of God abideth in him."

Resurrection cannot be equated with salvation as the Bible teaches it. All men will be resurrected: "And they [the dead] shall come forth; they that have done good, unto the resurrection of life; and they that have done evil, unto the resurrection of damnation" (John 5:29). To say that all men are saved because all are resurrected is to directly contradict the Word of God.

All men are resurrected, but those who believe in Christ and have been saved are resurrected 1000 years before the wicked dead. *None* in this first resurrection is lost. All these were saved through personally receiving Jesus as their Lord and Saviour. The wicked dead will be resurrected 1000 years later. None of the saved will be in the second resurrection. *All* those in the second resurrection will have rejected Christ and His salvation and they all will be lost (see Rev. 20:5,6). Two resurrections are clearly taught in the Bible. In the first resurrection *all* are saved! In the second resurrection, 1000 years later, *all* are lost!

Personal Salvation

The second part of the Mormon salvation is personal salvation, sometimes called individual or conditional salvation or exaltation. This salvation comes by grace plus baptism plus works.

Talmage says in *Articles of Faith,* "Redemption from personal sins can only be obtained through obedience to the

132

requirement of the Gospel, and a life of good works."[2]

Can you imagine quoting that to the thief on the cross as he was dying? Thank God, Christ was there and not Mr. Talmage, or the thief would have been forever lost.

We have asked Mormons and other devotees of works for salvation, how many good works we had to do to be sure of our salvation. No one knows. Surely, if works in any degree were necessary, God would have prominently and repeatedly listed how many, what they are, and guaranteed us the certainty of our salvation when we had done them all. This isn't God's way. When the religious Jews thought they could be saved, or help themselves be saved by good works, they asked Jesus, "What shall we do, that we might work the works of God? Jesus answered and said unto them, This is the work of God, that ye believe on him whom he hath sent" (John 6:28,29). No single work or large amount of works will ever bring salvation.

A man may keep 1000 good laws during his lifetime and never break one of them. He may also do 1000 good works in addition to this. However, if he breaks one law, no matter how significant or insignificant it may be, he must pay for it. A lifeguard may save 20 lives over a period of time. But if he deliberately and maliciously murders a man, he must face the penalty for his crime. The lives he saved in no way pay for the life he took.

Imagine someone running a red light, and being pulled over to the side by a policeman. And he says, "Hey, officer, you can't do a thing to me for going through that red light!"

The officer pushes his cap back on his head, sighs, and wonders if this is going to be one of those days. "O yeah," he answers noncommittally, "Why not?"

"Because I've driven through here at least a thousand times before and always stopped for the red light. I've kept the law 1000 times and broken it once. My good works outnumber my bad works 1000 to 1. Actually, you should reward me! You can't do a thing to me!"

Oh no? Try that approach some time and see how far you get. Would the law buy that facetious argument? Neither will God!

God's Salvation

In the first place, God cannot accept good works from a bad source, and He declares that all men are sinners, and therefore *lost*: "For all have sinned, and come short of the glory of God" (Rom. 3:23). It is not a matter of how far short each individual has come, but that *all* men have sinned and come short of the glory of God.

If every person were attempting to leap a 100-foot chasm, with a 10,000 foot drop to jagged rocks below, it would be purely academic as to how far some leaped, and how pitiful the efforts of others were. *All* would fail and be doomed because they were short of the mark, and that is God's point.

Not only that, but good works from an unrepentant heart are contaminated, and are not considered good by God at all. In fact, Isaiah said, "All our righteousnesses are as filthy rags!" (64:6) If all our righteousnesses are as filthy rags to God, what an insult it must be to Him for us to try to buy our salvation with them. Many filthy rags would be even more insulting than a few.

God sent Jesus to die in bloody agony on the cross to totally pay for all our sins. How it must hurt Him when we insist on hanging the dirty rags of our good works on the cross to "help Jesus save us" rather than accepting this great gift of salvation.

The problem is deeper than just the sins we commit, however. The real problem is the *sin-nature* every human being inherited from Adam. This is the sin-factory that keeps producing sin. Not all factories produce the same kind of sin, and not all factories produce the same amount of sin. Some sins are gross, some are socially acceptable, even highly regarded in some circles. All are abominable to God. If we allow bottles to represent the sin produced by these sin-factories, we might spend a lifetime destroying the bottles in a losing effort. The factory is still there, and though on occasion it may change the form or the brand of the product or slow down or speed up production, it is the same old sin-factory.

God says, in John 1:12, that the problem is that we are not children of God. Men by nature are *not* children of God! "But as many as received him, to them gave he power to become the sons of God, even to them that believe on his name."

Now God would not ask us to *become* children of God if we already *were* children of God. He plainly says we have to receive Jesus in order to become children of God. He told religious but lost Nicodemus, "Ye must be born again" (John 3:7).

We are born again into the family of God by receiving Jesus Christ as our personal Lord and Saviour. We call believingly on Him to forgive us our sins, and come into our heart and life and make us children of God. This is the personal invitation He is waiting for. He immediately enters our life, washing away our sins through His shed blood, and gives us his free gift of everlasting life.

At the same time, He gives us a new nature as a child of God, and He begins to live His life through us, insuring a changed life. Then and only then, *after* we are saved, are our good works of any value to God whatsoever. Then and only then, *after* we are saved, for the first time God truly becomes our father. He is not the Father of all men. He is the Father only of the saved, those born-again into the family of God through receiving Christ. Of the unsaved God says: "Ye are of your father the devil" (John 8:44). (See 1 John 3:8.)

Can you imagine a pig trying desperately to become a sheep by imitating a sheep? Suppose the pig became fed up with being a pig and noticed the sheep rambling about in the nice green pasture eating dry, clean, sheep food instead of slop. The pig manages to break out of the pig pen, find a dead sheep and clothe itself in the sheep wool. The pig learns to eat sheep feed, and slowly, agonizingly learns to bleat or talk sheep talk: "Oink, Bloink, Blah-h, Baa-a!"

Would the pig now be a sheep? Would it even be any closer to being a sheep? Would any of this change its basic pig nature? Would it matter in the slightest whether or not it was a "good" pig or a "bad" pig, by pig standards? Surely, we can all understand that a pig cannot become a sheep by acting like a sheep.

By the same token, no one can become a Christian by acting like a Christian. It does not matter how many "good" works or imitation Christian works we do, we can only become children of God by personally receiving Christ and being born again into God's family. Acting like a Christian, performing religious and other good works, is futile for salvation. We must be born again, and receive a new nature from God as children of God. Then, we will do good works for God, not in order to become Christians, but *because* we already are! (See Eph. 2:10.)

Faith Versus Works

Another rather obvious problem in working for our salvation in any degree is that God says of all men (unless they accept Christ and receive life through Him) that they are "dead in trespasses and sins" (Eph. 2:1). Just how much work can a dead man do, anyway?

It is true that in Christ, but only in *Christ,* are men made alive. Those in Christ have been made new creatures, with a new nature, new life, new desires, new power: "Therefore, if any man be in Christ, he is a new creature: old things are passed away; behold, all things are become new" (2 Cor. 5:17).

Mormons claim that in order to be able to claim personal salvation one must have faith in the Lord Jesus Christ, testify that Joseph Smith was a prophet of God, repent, be baptized into the Mormon church (the one true church) undergo the laying on of hands and keep the commandments. However, even after obeying all these requirements and believing there are three heavens and almost no hell, many Mormons are still fearful and uncertain. They admit they really don't know for sure where they will go when they die!

There is one and only one salvation taught in Scripture, and God says it is never gained by works. The first step anyone makes toward salvation is repentance of sin: "All we like sheep have gone astray; we have turned every one to his own way; and the Lord hath laid on him the iniquity of us all" (Isa. 53:6). Repentance in the Greek is *metanoia*, and simply means a change of mind about sin, self and Saviour. It is turning from going one's own way to going God's way. Repentance occurs simultaneously with salvation when one turns from sin to the Saviour.

Sin is basically following our old sin-nature, going our own way, being self-centered instead of Christ-centered. It is being the god, the lord, the boss of our own life. It is managing our own affairs rather than submitting control to God. God cannot permit rival gods, however benevolent they may at first seem, anywhere in His universe. Rebellion and chaos would be the ultimate result. Salvation consists in receiving Jesus by faith and going God's way rather than our own.

Ephesians 2:8,9 makes it crystal clear: "For by grace are ye *saved* through *faith*; and that not of yourselves: it is the gift of God: *not of works,* lest any man should boast" (italics added).

We are saved, *not by works, not by works, not by works, not by works*!

The Mormon answer is to try to nullify this clear and unmistakable statement. They turn rapidly to James 2:20: "But wilt thou know, O vain man, that faith without works is dead." How true! The devils have a head belief and they are in hell forever (see Jas. 2:19). It takes a heart belief (the ruling, governing, choosing center of man's being; see Rom. 10:9,10) to save a man. Saving faith, if it is real, always produces good works, not in order to be saved, but as proof that one *has been* saved. Faith without works never lived!

In James 2:18 we are told to show our faith by our works. We cannot show something we don't already have, and if we have faith we have already been saved. James is pointing out that all the talk about faith in the world is useless if one does not have a changed life proving he has truly been saved. James is telling us to demonstrate our salvation.

James goes on and tells about Abraham and how he was justified by *works* (v. 21), but he *believed* God and it was accounted to him for righteousness (v. 23; see also Gen. 15:6). What is the answer? Abraham was justified in the sight of God by his faith. He was justified in the sight of men by his works. Men can't see faith, they can only see the works that saving faith produces.

Fourteen years after Abraham believed God he was circumcised as an outward sign of the covenant he already had with God. He had been saved 14 years *before* he was circumcised (see Gen. 17:9-11).

Then, around 40 years or so *after* he had believed God and been saved (many years before the birth of Isaac) Abraham *proved* his faith before men. He demonstrated his salvation, as James points out, by faithfully offering his son Isaac upon the altar (see Gen. 22). Here we see how faith that does not produce a changed life is dead. Faith that does not produce works that justify our claims of salvation is not saving faith at all.

Incidentally, dramatic transformation of character and life is the norm in evangelical Christianity. Mel Trotter was an alcoholic. All his desperate promises and efforts to quit proved in vain.

One sad and dreary day, his precious little baby died. In his grief the insatiable craving for whiskey filled his being, but Mel was abysmally broke. Finally in self-loathing but in abject desperation, he slipped up to the casket where the cold body of his little baby lay. His fingers trembled as he tore the shoes from the tiny little feet. Then he shuffled out to sell the shoes for money to buy a drink.

Some time later, Mel met Jesus Christ as his personal Lord and Saviour and was *instantly* and *forever* changed. He became a devout Christian, his thirst quenched by the Saviour. In the following years he founded over 60 missions to preach Christ to needy men and women.

Where, by the way, are the *Mormon missions on skid row*? Where are the alcoholics, prostitutes, murderers, drug addicts, who can testify to being instantly saved and changed by Mormonism? Of course, every program, whether religious or secular, educational or rehabilitational, can claim favorable results in rehabilitating these needy people, but we are talking about the change that takes place in a few minutes and lasts forever that only Christ can make. I have seen this transformation again and again, in a few moments, as people receive Christ. Changes in lifetime habits, in disposition, attitudes, temper, a sudden and imperishable certainty about salvation, death and heaven. A sudden influx of love and concern for others, whether in psychologists, lawyers, businessmen, prostitutes, alcoholics, farmers, drug addicts, fishermen, miners, Alaskan guides, school teachers, housewives or whoever.

To work for our salvation, then, insults God and puts us further in *debt*. He wants us to *work out*, demonstrate our salvation, *after* we have been saved. (See Phil. 2:12.)

It is difficult to see how words concerning works for salvation could be clearer than these God gave in Romans 11:5,6: "Even so then at this present time also there is a remnant according to the election of grace. And if by grace, then is it no more of works: otherwise grace is no more grace. But if it be of works, then is it no more grace: otherwise work is no more work."

Biblical grace is God's unmerited love and salvation extended to the *totally undeserving,* without works. Look at the thief on the cross again—no church, no baptism, no good works, just sin, sin, sin. Then this hopeless wretch calls on Jesus Christ, "Lord, remember me when thou comest into thy kingdom. And Jesus said unto him, Verily I say unto thee, To day shalt thou be with me in paradise" (Luke 23:42,43). Instant salvation! Full and free! No works, no church, no baptism, nothing but faith, asking and believing Jesus! Without doubt, the thief would have had a changed life had he come down from the cross, but as a result of, not the means to, his salvation.

Contrast this with the Mormon teaching on grace. Mormon grace consists in part of doing religious, church and temple good works and so *making oneself worthy* of the grace of God. Read again the statement quoted previously in this chapter from Talmage's *Articles of Faith*: "Redemption from personal sins can only be obtained through obedience to the requirements of the Gospel and a life of good works."

Here is why Mormon grace is false and why works can *never* get one to heaven: "For if Abraham were justified by works, he hath whereof to glory; but not before God. For what saith the scripture? Abraham believed God, and it was counted unto him for righteousness. Now to him that worketh [for salvation] is the reward not reckoned of *grace,* but of *debt.* But to him that worketh not, but *believeth* on him that justifieth the ungodly, his faith is counted for righteousness" (Rom. 4:2-5).

We feel we must repeat, sadly, but with total conviction, *the Mormon religion is an elaborate doctrine of works, which denies the sufficiency of Christ alone to save.*

Christ, plus *nothing* saves. Christ, plus *nothing,* keeps us saved (once we fully commit ourselves by faith for salvation to Him). Anything else, the Bible declares to be heresy. Works follow salvation as proof of real salvation and to glorify Christ.

Footnotes

1. Stephen L. Richards, *Contributions of Joseph Smith* (Salt Lake City: The Church of Jesus Christ of Latter-day Saints).
2. Talmage, *Articles of Faith,* pp. 85, 87, 478, 479.

CHAPTER FOURTEEN

Biblical Salvation

A short time ago, in the predominantly Mormon field where we are now sharing our Saviour, we gave a young Mormon lady and her Mormon husband much of the material contained in this book. He was not interested enough to read it thoroughly, but she was.

At two o'clock in the morning, she could stand it no longer. She shook her husband awake and told him she wanted to be saved. He shrugged her off and told her to shut up and go back to sleep. She called me as soon as she could.

As we knelt together she poured out her heart, confessed her lostness, her sin, and took Jesus as her Saviour and Lord. She reveled in coming from the darkness of Mormonism to the light of Christ. Within two months she virtually committed the Gospel of Matthew to memory, learning and understanding more Scripture in a few weeks as a Christian, than in all her life before as a Mormon.

We have discovered that there is no division of salvation into "general" and "personal" salvation. There is only one salvation, and that comes by receiving the Lord Jesus Christ.

Mormons and Biblical Salvation

Following are true experiences (although some of the names

are fictitious) of Mormons who received this one salvation.

Tim O'Flannigan grew up in the Mormon church. His parents, now grown old, are still in the church. Youth activities were fun, and he readily absorbed the Mormon teaching both before and after his baptism into the Mormon church.

In spite of his Mormon testimony Tim began to drink and let other sins slip into his life. Marriage to breathtakingly lovely Jean, and the subsequent arrival of two precious children, should have quelled his restlessness, but they did not.

Jean was led to Jesus Christ by the sweet, consistent witness of a girl friend. Tim could not help but notice the change in her life but thought the last thing in the world he needed was "religion." He had plenty of that. Jean soon started coming to our church where she blossomed like a spring rose for Jesus Christ. Tim and I talked about his relationship with Christ. At first, he saw little difference in Mormon teaching and what the Bible said about salvation. Sometimes, he felt sure that he would go to heaven—well, one of the Mormon's three heavens anyway.

For awhile he avoided me, but he could not avoid the impact of the Word of God and the sweet testimony of his wife's changed life. Secretly, Tim had to admit that there was something different, alive, far more real and vibrant about Jean's life and testimony than there was about the life and testimony of the many Mormons he knew so well. Turmoil filled Tim's heart. Undeniably, the Bible taught that salvation was a *gift*; Mormonism taught that you had to work for your salvation. Which was right? Verses like Romans 4:5, "But to him that worketh not, but believeth on him that justifieth the ungodly, his faith is counted for righteousness," smote him like a sledgehammer.

Tim surrendered. He called on Jesus Christ to save him from his sins and fill the empty spot in his heart Mormonism never was able to fill. Jesus came into his heart, and Tim knew the testimony of joy and peace only the living Saviour can give, so different from his former Mormon testimony. Immediately, after his salvation, Tim turned from Mormonism to follow Christ in baptism in our church. Christ forever filled that empty spot.

I recently received a letter a young LDS mother wrote after reading some of the material in this book and after I visited her. In the letter she said: "I have seen things happen that I never thought could or would. *It is beautiful.* I'm real glad you came, and God is part of my life now. I pray that God will help you reach more LDS people to know and understand the love of God. It really distresses me to think some of the most beautiful people I know may not be in heaven because of this false and hypocritical way the LDS teaches....I am now a true born-again child of God the Lord. What a beautiful feeling is with me each new day. I know thru the love and faith of God I'll be able to overcome my old teachings. Thanks again for helping me see the light."

Later, I had the joy of returning to her town, and leading her husband to Jesus Christ.

Brett Somers was a rather well-to-do Mormon, with a beautiful home, in Washington state. Both he and his wife were very active in the Mormon church. After years of faithful, even brilliant service in the Mormon church, Mrs. Somers became increasingly troubled about the lack of vital interest in talking about Jesus Christ she found among church leaders, officials, and her Mormon women friends. What she heard the leaders say and what she read in the Bible did not seem to agree. She dug deeply into the *Book of Mormon,* and other Mormon books, seeking to bolster her once flaming faith. She read carefully through the *Articles of Faith,* by Talmage, marking many passages. (I know! She gave me the book!)

I was holding evangelistic meetings in the vicinity and Mrs. Somers made an appointment with me. She asked me very careful, intelligent questions about Mormonism, the Bible and salvation. She took home some of the material I have included in this book. She asked the Christ of the *Bible,* not of *Mormonism,* into her heart. Now she clearly, definitely, recommitted her life to Christ and made up her mind to leave the Mormon church.

Brett was in a quandary. Some of his wife's searchings had begun to trouble him. He went with her for a little while to an evangelical church. But he was a Mormon! Where was the answer?

God graciously opened the way for me to have an appointment with Brett. Slowly, carefully, prayerfully, I presented the gospel to Brett and answered questions from the Word of God, the Bible. Finally, I said, "Brett, Jesus loves you so much. He died for you and promises that if you call on Him to save you from your sins, He will do it. Brett, will you call on Jesus Christ to save you, right now?"

Brett bowed his head, and simply, quietly invited the risen Christ to come into his life and save him from his sins. Oh, the unspeakable joy and radiance that shone from his tear-filled eyes as he lifted them to mine! I showed several Bible verses, such as Romans 10:13 and John 3:36, to him again and he quickly memorized and claimed John 3:36.

Then I asked Brett if he *knew* beyond the shadow of a doubt that Jesus had saved him and given him the wonderful gift of everlasting life. Brett gave a resounding Yes. We prayed together and Brett thanked the Lord Jesus Christ for saving him from his sins, from Mormonism, and from hell.

Brett and his wife were, by their request, excommunicated from the Mormon church and are very active in a Baptist church and vitally concerned about leading others to Christ. Now both Brett and his wife know what a real testimony for Jesus Christ is. They can't keep quiet about *Him*!

Some of the names in these testimonies are fictitious to protect the individuals involved. No one, who has not experienced it, can believe the intense pressure the Mormon church, Mormon leaders, relatives, loved ones, family and friends, can

144

put on those who get saved and leave the Mormon church.

However the names in the following experience are true. Janet Webster printed and widely circulated her 12-page testimony.

Janet is a very lively lady and was an enthusiastic Mormon. She was in the process of acting as a missionary to two very good Christian friends, teaching them the six missionary lessons. Janet was sure her friends would soon see the "truth of the Mormon church," especially if they knew "of all its wonderful, beautiful, and glorious principles and doctrines." However, when she looked in the Bible for one of the Scriptures Mormons use to try to prove a doctrine, she found, to her chagrin and astonishment, that she had to read what the Bible said before and after the Scripture to understand its complete meaning! This one experience led her to read more and more of the Bible and she became convinced it was God's perfect Word, and she saw her need for Jesus Christ. She accepted Him as her Lord and Saviour and turned from Mormonism forever.

She said in her letter, "How can I tell you of the blessed miracle which has happened to our family? By the marvelous, wonderful grace of God, we have been called out from darkness and redeemed by our precious Lord and Saviour, Jesus Christ."

Janet's daughter, Brenda, a student at Brigham Young University, came home to her "apostate," newly-Christian family. In time, the love of Christ and Christians won, and Brenda met Christ also.

Janet wrote cogently, "Suddenly it came into sharp focus ... there are two camps (or sides) on this earth. On the first side, we have those who unreservedly uphold the Word of God (Bible), trusting it completely. And on the second side are those who would (and do) undermine (sometimes subtly) the Bible and proclaim that the Bible is not a supernatural book. Instead they believe their own intellectual ideas or scientific

145

knowledge (Atheists), or new prophets and Scriptures (Spiritualists, Jehovah Witnesses, Mormons, Bahai, Science and Mind, etc.) are to be trusted over the Bible. Well, why not, you say? I can only tell you why not for me. First, please notice that there are many groups in the second camp, but there is only one group in the first: *born again Christians,* who feel there is no salvation in any particular denomination, or in following a prophet, or Pope, etc., but only in and through Jesus Christ. And Jesus Christ and Him crucified *only* do they preach. These Christians all belong to the same church—the church of Jesus Christ, even though they fellowship in many different denominations...."

Janet went on to say that it was a glaring revelation to her as a Mormon, before she was converted to Christ, that she was in the same camp with atheists and all the other cults, who did not believe in the sufficiency or accuracy of the Bible. She realized the fallacy of the Mormon teaching, "We believe the Bible to be the Word of God as far as it is translated correctly."

Janet declared that she once thought Christians who believed they were saved by grace were given a free license to sin all they wanted to. Now, she knows how untrue this is. "How glorious it is to obey the Lord, not to gain salvation or exaltation, but just because you love the Lord, and knowing that because He died for you, your greatest desire in life is to live for Him! That can't compare with the idea of offering our puny works in exchange for exaltation."

She adds, "This is what *believing on Jesus* really means! It means that you believe Him when He tells us that the wages of sin is death, and so if we are going to be punished for our own sins (even one little unrepented sin), that means death—*spiritual death! Believing on Jesus* means we believe Him when He tells us He has died and paid in full the penalty for our sins and therefore, we will not be punished for our sins! And *believing on Jesus* means that you believe Him when He tells you that you must *accept Him as your* (personal) *Saviour.*"

Three days after Janet accepted Jesus Christ as her Saviour she knew for sure that the Mormon church was wrong, and she left it. She now has the wonderful joy of having seen God bring her family to Jesus Christ.

More than Head Belief

Does salvation actually work? For nominal Christians who may be religious but have only a head belief in Christ, the answer is definitely no! Unfortunately, many churches have members who are nominal Christians. I was a nominal Christian. On such the cultists feed.

For those who turn believingly to Jesus Christ with all their heart, the answer is a thrilling, resounding yes!

I owe a debt to the Mormons and to John, my Mormon friend, mentioned in the first chapter. Because of John, I discovered that my head religion was not enough. I truly came to know Christ as my personal Lord and Saviour. Now, I want to share Him with you.

God loves all of us so very much, so much that He sent Christ to shed His blood on the cross for us. Even more to the point God loves you. Will you turn away from sin and self to the Saviour? God says we are all sinners, and that means we are *all lost*. You will never be truly saved, till you admit that you are lost! Until you can admit that, you insult God, and accuse Him of letting His Son die for you when there was no need!

Exactly how do I turn to Christ? "As many as received him, to them gave he power to become the sons of God, even to them that believe on his name" (John 1:12). You must confess to God that you are a lost sinner, and receive Jesus Christ as your Saviour. Instantly, He will save you and you will be born again a child of God with a new nature.

How do I receive Him? Accept Jesus as the eternal God who is bodily resurrected from the dead. You must "confess with thy mouth the Lord [God, Boss, new Manager of your life]

147

Jesus [Saviour from sin and hell], and shalt believe in thine heart that God hath raised him from the dead, [then] thou shalt [absolutely, not maybe!] be saved" (Rom. 10:9).

What do I do to receive Him? Call with all your heart, believingly on Him! "For whosoever shall call upon the name of the Lord shall be saved" (Rom. 10:13). If you call believingly, Jesus will *have* to save you or He would be lying, because He promised. He cannot lie! Besides, if He loved you enough to die in broken, bloody, lonely agony on a cruel cross, would He turn you down when you call on Him to save you? Of course not!

Simply pray: "Lord Jesus Christ, please save me from all my sins. Cleanse me by your shed blood. Give me your free gift of everlasting life. Come into my heart and life right now. Make me a child of God, and let me know that I am saved, now and forever. I now receive you as my very own personal Lord and Saviour."

The Christ you are receiving is the eternal Christ, who always has been and always will be God, from everlasting to everlasting.

Did Christ save you—not according to your feelings but according to the Word of God? Then simply thank Him out loud for saving your soul and giving you eternal life.

Memorize, right now, the first part of John 3:36, "He that believeth on the Son hath [right now] everlasting life." So, the moment you believed, God said He gave you everlasting life!

Find a church that teaches the blood of Christ and makes salvation clear, and believes the Bible and the Bible alone. Join it, and attend regularly as God commands true Christians in Hebrews 10:25.

Follow Christ in baptism to show the world that your sins were washed away when you were saved (see Acts 10:47,48), and to show that you are dead to the old life and resurrected with Him to the new life.

Read slowly through the Gospel of John. Confess to others

that Christ has saved you. Share Christ constantly with others (see Acts 1:8). The greatest responsibility and joy in all the world, other than being saved, is leading others to know Christ!

Pray often, and tell Jesus every day that you love Him and thank Him for dying on the cross for you and for saving you! If you sin, confess it instantly, whether in thought, word or deed and thank God for His instant forgiveness (see 1 John 1:9). A Christian can sin, but a true Christian cannot continue to live habitually in sin. Let Christ live this new life through you. Tell Him you love Him and daily give Him permission to live His life each day through you.

Come out of Mormonism if you care about your soul, and the souls of others you will influence either for heaven or hell. "For what shall it profit a man, if he shall gain the whole world, and lose his own soul?" (Mark 8:36).

If you are truly saved, God says you will obey Him: "Jesus answered and said unto him, If a man love me, he will keep my words: and my Father will...come unto him, and make our abode with him" (John 14:23).

Do not be overly concerned about feelings. God wants you to walk by faith, not by feelings and sometimes He will completely remove all feelings to see if you are going to walk by faith in Him and in His Word. At other times there may be inexpressible joy and peace, but feelings or not, His Word is true.

Here is a valuable illustration. Three men waiting on the first floor, want to go to the seventh floor of a building. One is laughing, one is crying, and one is stoical. Their feelings do not matter at all. What matters is that they all trust the elevator to get them to the seventh floor. So they step into it and commit themselves to it, and the elevator takes all of them to the seventh floor.

So it is with coming to Christ. It does not matter greatly whether you cry or laugh or have little or no feeling. If you

149

trust Christ to save you and step by faith into Him, and commit yourself to Him, He will get you to heaven as He promised, feelings or no feelings. But the very realization that one has been truly saved from sin and from eternal hell, sooner or later, will bring a sense of relief and peace, but not always at the very moment of salvation.

Just as you must take medicine before it can take effect, so must you trust Christ and His Word, after calling on Him, before He can give you more feelings of joy, peace and His love than you ever dreamed possible.

Here are some verses you may want to learn. In any event they will be very helpful to you in your Christian life.

Acts 1:8: "But ye shall receive power, after that the Holy Ghost is come upon you: and ye shall be witnesses unto me both in Jerusalem, and in all Judea, and in Samaria, and unto the uttermost part of the earth."

First John 1:9: "If we confess our sins, he is faithful and just to forgive us our sins, and to cleanse us from all unrighteousness."

First John 3:14: "We know that we have passed from death unto life, because we love the brethren. He that loveth not his brother abideth in death."

How God loves us! It is my prayer that I have not hindered His love from flowing through me, even though God led me to point out the errors in Mormonism. God loves the Mormon people, and, as far as I know my heart, so do I. God does not love Mormonism, which teaches people about another God, another Jesus, to their eternal loss.

If this book has been a blessing to you, please share it with as many people as you can in this desperate day of darkness and incredible urgency. Pray much for its use for Jesus, and for souls for Him.

Appendix: The Way to Salvation

Dr. Norman Lewis of Western Conservative Baptist Seminary, Portland, Oregon states that every true Christian is confronted with the "inescapable command" to witness to all men without Christ.

"Go ye therefore, and teach all nations, baptizing them in the name of the Father, and of the Son, and of the Holy Ghost: Teaching them to observe all things whatsoever I have commanded you: and, lo, I am with you alway, even unto the end of the world" (Matt. 28:19,20).

"But ye shall receive power, after that the Holy Ghost is come upon you: and ye shall be witnesses unto me both in Jerusalem, and in all Judea, and in Samaria, and unto the uttermost part of the earth" (Acts 1:8).

When you combine this great admonition with John 14:23, "Jesus answered and said unto him, If a man love me, he will keep my words," truly the responsibility to share Christ with all men, including Mormons, is inescapable. If we love Jesus, if we believe men are lost, if we believe in heaven and hell, we *must* share with Mormon friends as well as with others who need Jesus.

Following are questions that will show you, dear Mormon friends, the way to salvation.

(Italicized words in quoted passages are added by the author.)

1. The Bible says there is only *one* God who created all universes, planets and worlds. Joseph Smith and other Mormon leaders teach that there are many Gods. Which do you believe?

The Bible

"*Before* me there was no God formed, neither shall there be *after* me" (Isa. 43:10).

"Is there a God beside me? Yea, there is no God; I know not any" (Isa. 44:8).

Mormon Writers

"And the *Gods* ordered, saying: let the waters under the heaven be gathered together unto one place, and let the earth come up dry; and it was so as they ordered; and the gathering together of the waters pronounced they, great waters; and the *Gods* saw that they were obeyed" (Joseph Smith, *Pearl of Great Price,* Abraham 4:9,10; published by The Church of Jesus Christ of Latter-day Saints, Salt Lake City, Utah, 1967).

"If we should take a million of worlds like this and number their particles, we should find that there are more Gods than there are particles of matter in those worlds" (Orson Pratt, *Journal of Discourses,* vol. 2; published by F. D. & S. W. Richards, Liverpool, 1854; reprint ed. Salt Lake City, Utah, 1966, p. 345).

Comment

Obviously, God declares there never has been, is not now, and never will be any other God in this or any other world, on this or any other planet.

For additional information see chapter 7, "The Fatal Flaw," in this book.

2. The Bible teaches that God *never* originated as a man, that He was God from all eternity past. The Bible also teaches that there will *never* be any other God. Mormonism teaches that God was once a man *before* He became God. Mormonism also teaches that men may someday become Gods. Which do you believe?

The Bible

"From everlasting to everlasting, *thou art God*" (Ps. 90:2).

"For I am God, and not man" (Hos. 11:9).

"I am the first, and I am the last; and *beside me there is no God*" (Isa. 44:6).

Mormon Writers

"God himself was once as we are now and is an exalted *man,* and sits enthroned in yonder heavens!" (Joseph Smith, *Teachings of Prophet Joseph Smith*; published by Deseret Book Co., Salt Lake City, 1969, p. 345).

"Remember that God our Heavenly Father was perhaps once a child, and *mortal* like we are and rose step by step in the scale of progress, in the school of advancement" (Orson Hyde, *Journal of Discourses,* vol. 1, p. 123; published by F. D. and S. W. Richards, Liverpool, 1854; reprint ed. Salt Lake City, Utah, 1966).

"The Lord created you and me for the purpose of becoming *Gods like Himself*" (Brigham Young, *Journal of Discourses,* vol. 3, p. 93).

"As man is, God once was; as God is, man may be" (Lorenzo Snow, former President of the Mormon church, *Millenial Star,* vol. 54; also Milton R. Hunter, *The Gospel Through the Ages,* pp. 105,106).

Comment

According to the Bible, God never progressed His way into being God, He always was God. Clearly man did not exist prior to God. Clearly too, since God declares there will *never* be any other God, men will *never* become gods.

For additional information see chapter 8, "Contradictions Concerning the Person of God," in this book.

3. The Bible teaches that Jesus Christ *always* was God from eternity past. Mormonism teaches that there was a time when Jesus Christ was *not* God. Which do you believe?

The Bible

"But thou, Bethlehem Ephratah, though thou be little among the thousands of Judah, yet out of thee shall he come forth unto me that is to be ruler in Israel: whose goings forth have been from old, *from everlasting*" (Mic. 5:2).

"In the beginning *was* the Word [Jesus], and the Word was with God, and the Word *was God*" (John 1:1).

"Before Abraham was, *I am*" (John 8:58).

Mormon Writers

"Christ the Word, the First born, had of course *attained* unto the status of Godhood while yet in pre-existence" (booklet, *What the Mormons Think of Christ*; published by The Church of Jesus Christ of Latter-day Saints, p. 336).

"Jesus *became a* God and reached His great state of understanding through consistent effort and continuous obedience to all the Gospel truths and universal laws" (Milton R. Hunter, *The Gospel Through the Ages*; published by Deseret Book Co., Salt Lake City, 1945, p. 51).

Comment

God was God from the beginning, from all time, and so was

Jesus Christ God from the beginning, *from all time.* Jesus Christ *always was and is God.* Jesus told Phillip, in John 14:9, "He that hath seen me hath seen the Father."

For additional information see chapter 7, "The Fatal Flaw," under the subhead, *The Christ,* in this book.

4. Deuteronomy 18:20-22 says that God's test for a prophet includes 100% accuracy in fulfillment of his prophecies, or the prophet is a false prophet. Many of Joseph Smith's prophecies were never fulfilled. According to the biblical test, was Joseph Smith a true prophet or a false prophet?

The Bible

"But the prophet, which shall presume to speak a word in my name, which I have not commanded him to speak, or that shall speak in the name of other gods, even that prophet shall die. And if thou say in thine heart, How shall we know the word which the Lord hath not spoken? When a prophet speaketh in the name of the Lord, *if the thing follow not, nor come to pass,* that is the thing which the Lord hath not spoken, but the prophet hath spoken it presumptuously: thou shalt not be afraid of him" (Deut. 18:20-22).

Mormon Writers

Prophecy given by Joseph Smith, September 1832: New Jerusalem and its Temple are to be built in Missouri *in this generation* (Joseph Smith, *Doctrine and Covenants* 84:1-5; published by The Church of Jesus Christ of Latter-day Saints, 1968).

"The Latter-day Saints just as much expect to see a fulfillment of that promise during the *generation that was then in existence in 1832* as they expect that the sun will rise and set tomorrow. Why? Because God cannot lie. *He will fulfill all His promises*" (Apostle Orson Pratt, *Journal of Discourses,* vol. 9; published by F. D. and S. W. Richards, Liverpool, 1854; reprint ed. Salt Lake City, 1966, p. 71).

This prophecy was not fulfilled, therefore it is *false.*

Prophecy given by Joseph Smith sometime between 1831 and 1844: Nauvoo House to be built and to belong to the Smith family forever (Joseph Smith, *Doctrine and Covenants* 124:56-60; published by The Church of Jesus Christ of Latter-day Saints, 1968). Smith was killed in 1844 and the Mormons were driven from Nauvoo. The house no longer belongs to the Smith family. The prophecy was *false.*

Prophecy by Joseph Smith: "The coming of the Lord which was nigh... *even 56 years should wind up the scene*" (Joseph Smith, *History of the Church,* vol. 2, p. 182; published by Deseret News Publishers, Salt Lake City, 1902–1912). This prophecy was *false.*

Comment

Joseph Smith fails God's test for a true prophet. He was *not* a prophet of God.

For additional information see chapter 3, "Joseph Smith— Prophet of God?" in this book.

5. The Bible says that Christ was begotten by the Holy Spirit. Mormon prophet, Brigham Young, said Christ was *not* begotten by the Holy Ghost. Which do you believe?

The Bible

"For that which is conceived in her is of the Holy Ghost" (Matt. 1:20).

"The Holy Ghost shall come upon thee... therefore also that holy thing which shall be born of thee shall be called the Son of God" (Luke 1:35).

Mormon Writers

"The child Jesus... was not begotten by the Holy Ghost" (Brigham Young, *Journal of Discourses,* vol. 1; published by F. D. and S. W. Richards, Liverpool, 1854; reprint ed., Salt Lake City, Utah, 1966, pp. 50, 51).

Comment

Would a true prophet of God contradict the Word of God?

For additional information see chapter 7, "The Fatal Flaw," in this book.

6. The Bible teaches that God *made* Adam and gave him life. Brigham Young taught that Adam "is our father and our God and the *only* God with whom we have to do." Which do you believe?

The Bible

"And the Lord God *formed* man of the dust of the ground, and breathed into his nostrils the breath of life; and man became a living soul" (Gen. 2:7).

"For Adam was first *formed,* then Eve" (1 Tim. 2:13).

Mormon Writers

"When our father Adam came into the Garden of Eden, He came into it with a celestial body and brought Eve, *one* of his *wives,* with him. He helped to make and organize this world. He is Michael, the Arch-angel, the Ancient of Days! about whom holy men have written and spoken. He [Adam] is our Father and our God and the only God with whom we have to do" (Brigham Young, *Journal of Discourses*; vol. 1; published by F. D. and S. W. Richards, Liverpool, 1854; reprint ed. Salt Lake City, Utah, 1966, p. 50).

Comment

To deny the Adam-God doctrine is to admit that Brigham

Young is a false prophet. To accept it denies God's Word, the Bible.

For further information see chapter 8, "Contradictions Concerning the Person of God."

7. The Bible calls the study of genealogies foolish. Mormons make extensive use of genealogies in their system of works, baptizing for the dead, etc. Which do you believe is right?

The Bible
"But *avoid* foolish questions, and *genealogies,* and contentions, and strivings about the law; for they are *unprofitable* and *vain*" (Titus 3:9).

"Neither give *heed* to fables and endless *genealogies* which minister questions, rather than godly edifying which is in faith: so do" (1 Tim. 1:4).

Mormon Writers
"Before vicarious ordinances of salvation and exaltation may be performed for those who have died... they must be accurately and properly identified. Hence, *genealogical research* is required.... The Church maintains in Salt Lake City one of the world's greatest *genealogical societies.* Much of the genealogical source material of various nations of the earth has been or is being microfilmed by this society; *millions of dollars* are being spent; and a reservoir of *hundreds millions* of *names* and other data about people who lived in past generations is available for study (McConkie, *Mormon Doctrine*, pp. 308, 309).

Comment
Genealogical records were destroyed in Jerusalem in A.D. 70 by the Romans under Titus, underlining God's closing

the door on genealogies, since Jesus had come and fulfilled their purpose.

For additional information on genealogies, see chapter 9, "Priesthood and Genealogies" in this book.

8. The Bible, the Church and history cast strong doubt on the Mormon claim that they have "new" or "further" revelation. Which do you believe?

The Bible

"For I testify unto every man that heareth the words of the prophecy of this book, If any man shall add unto these things, God shall add unto him the plagues that are written in this book: And if any man shall take away from the words of the book of this prophecy, God shall take away his part out of the book of life, and out of the holy city, and from the things which are written in this book" (Rev. 22:18,19).

"I will build my church; and the gates of hell shall not prevail against it" (Matt. 16:18).

"Beware of false prophets, who come to you in sheep's clothing, but inwardly they are ravening wolves" (Matt. 7:15).

Mormon Writers

"On the morning of a beautiful spring day in 1820 there occurred one of the most important and momentous events in this world's history. God, the Eternal Father and His Son, Jesus Christ, appeared to Joseph Smith and gave instructions concerning the establishment of the kingdom of God upon the earth in these latter days" (LeGrand Richards, *A Marvelous Work and a Wonder*; Salt Lake City, Deseret Book Co., 1971, p. 7).

"Containing *Revelations* Given to Joseph Smith, Jr. The Prophet" (*Doctrine and Covenants*; published by The Church of Jesus Christ of Latter-day Saints, 1968, title page).

Comment

The book of Revelation gives us the picture of the church age, the tribulation, millennium, and the consummation of all things on into the eternal state, all time being fully covered. God did not "forget" anything that would make it necessary to add a divine PS by further revelation.

"This book" in Revelation 22:18,19, certainly seems to apply primarily to the book of Revelation. However, the all-knowing God who knows the future *certainly* knew which book would be placed at the end of the Bible, and that the Bible is and was referred to as a unit, or book. It seems more than a coincidence that the most powerful warning in the Bible concerning its words or adding to its prophecies should be on the *last* page, in the *last* chapter, of the *last* book of the Bible, by the *last* prophet, with the *last* true and certain prophecies.

Historically, no prophet has arisen since biblical days who can foretell the future with the 100% accuracy required of a true biblical prophet. *None,* since New Testament days, has met the test, proving conclusively that the prophetical gift of foretelling the future has been withdrawn, and that there is no "new" or further revelation from God.

For additional information see chapter 12, "The Final Authority," in this book.

9. Do you, as a Mormon, understand that opening the door to "new" or further "revelation," the truth of which is determined in part by "feeling," "testimony," or a "burning in the bosom," makes it possible for you or anyone else to claim revelations from God and construct any kind of teaching you want? Could you have confidence in a religion that is constructed from such "revelations"? Do you believe the word of a discredited "prophet" (one whose prophecies failed) who said he had "new" revelation, or do you believe the Bible?

The Bible

"But though we, or an *angel* from *heaven,* preach *any other gospel* unto you than *that which we have preached unto you,* let him be accursed" (Gal. 1:8).

"And no marvel; for Satan himself is transformed into an *angel of light.* Therefore it is no great thing if *his ministers also* be transformed as the *ministers of righteousness*; whose end shall be according to their works" (2 Cor. 11:14,15).

"Thy *Word* is a lamp unto my feet, and a *light* unto my path" (Ps. 119:105).

Mormon Writers

"I received the *First Visitation of Angels,* which was when I was about fourteen years old" (Joseph Smith, quoted in the *Deseret News,* May 29, 1852).

"By and by an obscure individual, a young man, rose up, and, in the midst of all Christendom, proclaimed the startling news that God had sent an *Angel* to him" (Orson Pratt, Apostle, *Journal of Discourses,* vol. 13; published by F. D. and S. W. Richards, Liverpool, 1854; reprint ed. Salt Lake City, Utah, 1966, pp. 65, 66).

"But behold, I say unto you, that you must study it out in your mind; then you must ask me if it be right, and if it is right I will cause that your bosom shall *burn* within you; therefore, you shall *feel* that is is right" (Joseph Smith, *Doctrine and Covenants* 9:8).

Comment

Here you see that the claims of Mormonism are similar to scores of others, such as Christian Science, that have added other "inspired" books and Rev. Moon of the Unification Church who claims he had a vision of Jesus in 1956. These teach that they have had further revelation, visits by angels, visions, etc., for the purpose of "understanding" or adding to Scripture. You also see that the proof they claim shifts your attention away from the Bible as full and final authority, so that anything goes.

Incidentally, no amount of "testimony," "burning in the bosom" or "feeling" can make Joseph Smith's prophecies come true, or turn a false prophet into a true prophet.

For additional information see chapter 12, "The Final Authority," in this book.

10. The Bible teaches that hell is eternal. Mormonism teaches that hell is not eternal punishment for all lost men. Which do you believe?

The Bible

"And these shall go away into everlasting punishment: but the righteous into life eternal" (Matt. 25:46).

"He that believeth on the Son hath everlasting life: and he that believeth not the Son shall not see life; but the wrath of God *abideth* on him" (John 3:36).

"And whosoever was not found written in the book of life was cast into the lake of fire" (Rev. 20:15).

Mormon Writers

"Eternal punishment is God's punishment: everlasting punishment is God's punishment; or in other words it is the *name* of the punishment God inflicts. He being eternal in his nature. Whosoever, therefore, receives God's punishment, receives eternal punishment whether it is endured one hour, one day, one week, one year, or an age" (Elder John Morgan, pamphlet, *The Plan of Salvation,* published by The Church of Jesus Christ of Latter-day Saints, 1970, p. 29).

"In The Church of Jesus Christ of Latter-day Saints, *there is no hell. All* will find a measure of salvation" (Apostle John Widtsoe, *Evidences and Reconciliations,* p. 216; same statement found in *Joseph Smith—Seeker After Truth,* Salt Lake City, 1951, pp. 177, 178).

Comment

The same Greek word from which everlasting and eternal are translated, *aionios,* is used to describe the eternal continuance of heaven, hell and God. If one is eternal all are. Revelation 14:11, picturing some of the lost already in hell, declares that they have "no rest night nor day," and that "the smoke of their torment ascendeth up forever and ever." The choice is clear, either the Bible or Mormon teaching. Mormon teaching.

For additional information, see chapter 10, "Some Distinctive but Dubious Doctrines of Mormonism," in this book.

11. The Bible teaches that David and Paul, both murderers, were forgiven and that "the blood of Jesus Christ, his Son, cleanses from *all sin.*" Joseph Smith's teachings say that murder is an unforgivable sin. Which do you believe?

The Bible

(After David confessed to murdering Uriah, and taking his wife, Bathsheba), "The Lord also hath put away thy sin; thou shalt not die" (2 Sam. 12:13).

"And Saul, yet breathing out threatenings and *slaughter* against the disciples of the Lord, went unto the high priest" (Acts 9:1).

"And I persecuted this way unto the *death,* binding and delivering into prisons both men and women" (Acts 22:4).

"The blood of Jesus Christ, his Son, cleanseth us from all sin" (1 John 1:7).

Mormon Writers

"And, now, behold, I speak unto the church. Thou shalt not kill; and he that kills shall not have forgiveness in this world, nor in the world to come" (Joseph Smith, *Doctrine and Covenants* 42:18; also 132:26, 27; published by The Church of

Jesus Christ of Latter-day Saints, 1968).

"Hopes of reward through so-called Deathbed repentance are vain" (Bruce McConkie, *Mormon Doctrine,* p. 631).

Comment

Saul was responsible for the death of Stephen and others. Yet Saul, the murderer, became Paul, the missionary, from one vital encounter with the risen Christ on the Damascus road. His sins were forgiven. He was cleansed by the blood of the Lord Jesus Christ.

For additional information see chapter 14, "Biblical Salvation," in this book.

12. The Bible teaches that *all men* are *lost sinners* needing salvation, and that only those who personally trust Christ are saved. Mormonism teaches that resurrection is salvation, and since all men will be resurrected, all men are therefore saved. They call this "general salvation." Which do you believe?

The Bible

"For all have sinned, and come short of the glory of God" (Rom. 3:23).

"And this is the will of him that sent me, that every one which seeth the Son, and believeth on him, may have everlasting life: and I will raise him up at the last day" (John 6:40).

"Jesus said unto her, I am the resurrection, and the life: he that believeth in me, though he were dead, yet shall he live: and whosoever liveth and believeth in me shall never die" (John 11:25).

"Believe on the Lord Jesus Christ, and thou shalt be saved" (Acts 16:31).

Mormon Writers

"There will be a General Salvation for *all* in the sense in which the term is generally used, but salvation, *meaning resurrection,* is not exaltation" (Stephen L. Richards, pamphlet, *Contributions of Joseph Smith,* published by The Church of Jesus Christ of Latter-day Saints, p. 5).

"*All* men are *saved* by grace alone without any act on their part, meaning they are *resurrected*" (Apostle Bruce McConkie, *What the Mormons Think of Christ,* p. 28, pamphlet currently published by The Church of Jesus Christ of Latter-day Saints).

Comment

Mormons equate salvation with resurrection. Everybody is *not* automatically saved whether he believes or not. Resurrection is not salvation. There will be a resurrection to damnation for those who do not believe as well as a resurrection to salvation (John 5:28,29; Acts 24:15).

For additional information see chapter 13, "Mormon Salvation," in this book.

13. The Bible says that all salvation is by faith alone in Jesus Christ alone. Mormonism teaches that by doing good works man must make himself "worthy" of individual or personal salvation. Which do you believe?

The Bible

"As it is written, There is *none righteous, no, not one*" (Rom. 3:10).

"For I bear them [unsaved, religious Jews] record that they have a zeal of God, but not according to knowledge. For they being ignorant of God's righteousness, and going about to establish their own righteousness, have not submitted themselves unto the righteousness of God" (Rom. 10:2,3).

"He that believeth on me hath everlasting life" (John 6:47).

"Wherefore he is able also to save them to the uttermost that come unto God by him, seeing he ever liveth to make intercession for them" (Heb. 7:25).

Mormon Writers

"For we know that it is by grace that we are saved, *after all we can do*" (Joseph Smith, *Book of Mormon,* 2 Nephi 25:23).

"Redemption from personal sins can only be obtained through obedience to the requirements of the gospel, and a *life of good works*" (James Talmage, *Articles of Faith,* published by The Church of Jesus Christ of Latter-day Saints, 1952, pp. 478, 479).

Comment

As stated and proven scripturally, Christ's blood cleanses from all sin, and He saves to the *uttermost,* and there is no salvation that is fuller, higher, greater or more wonderful!

Good works including baptism, come *after* a person has been saved. They demonstrate salvation and prove its reality. Never does God accept our good works as a means to salvation (see Eph. 2:8,9). Baptism is also a symbol that we have been saved, not a way by which we must be saved. Acts 10:44-48 says: "While Peter yet spake these words, the Holy Ghost fell on all them which heard the word.... Then answered Peter, Can any man forbid water, that these should not be baptized, which have received the Holy Ghost as well as we? And he commanded them to be baptized in the name of the Lord." The thief on the cross and the publican in the temple, Luke 18:9-14, were all saved without baptism.

For additional information see chapters 13 and 14.

14. The Bible teaches that we are sinners and must be born again to *become* children of God by receiving Christ. Mormonism teaches that we are all children of God. Which do you believe?

The Bible

"Except a man be born again, he cannot see the kingdom of God" (John 3:3).

"But as many as *received him,* to *them* gave he power *to become* the *sons* of *God,* even to them that believe on his name" (John 1:12).

Mormon Writers

"Man is in reality a child of God.... In the Mormon concept the phrase, the fatherhood of God and the brotherhood of man, takes on a new and powerful meaning" (Elder Gordon B. Hinckley, pamphlet, *What of The Mormons?*; published by The Church of Jesus Christ of Latter-day Saints, 1975, p. 6).

"All men and women are in the similitude of the universal Father and Mother, and are literally the sons and daughters of Deity" (Joseph Smith, *Man: His Origin and Destiny,* pp. 351, 355).

Comment

God would not tell us to *become* children by receiving Christ and being born again, if we *already were* by nature children of God.

For additional information see chapter 13, "Mormon Salvation," in this book.

15. The Bible says true Christians *can and do know* they are saved, here and now, and they are sure of going to heaven to be with Jesus forever. Can you, as a Mormon say that you are absolutely sure you have personal salvation right now. That you will go to the "highest" heaven to be with Jesus Christ forever? Christians *know.* Do you?

The Bible

"These things have I written unto you that believe on the

name of the Son of God; that ye may *know* that ye *have* eternal life, and that ye may believe on the name of the Son of God" (1 John 5:13).

"He that *hath* the Son *hath* life; and he that hath not the Son of God hath *not* life" (1 John 5:12).

Mormon Writers (Author's comment)

I have quoted many Mormon writers on the subject of good works for salvation. Since we can never know when we have done enough good works, or whether we are accepted of God, it is obvious that Mormons are very uncertain about true personal salvation. I have talked with scores of Mormons, high and low in the church, and almost none of them could claim they knew for sure that they would go the "highest" (really the only) heaven to be with Jesus Christ forever. If such a claim is made, it is usually qualified on the basis of continued good works, faithfulness to the Mormon church and ordinances, or just the general idea that since there are three heavens they surely should reach one of them. Really, Mormons do not know where they are going when they die. Their main hope is in the invention of a discredited Mormon prophet and his myth of three heavens or degrees of glory. They at least feel pretty sure they won't go to hell. However, all men will go either to heaven or hell, according to the Bible, and any other hope is a false hope.

16. The Bible tells us to beware of false Christs, and false prophets. According to Mormon prophets and writers, you as a Mormon are trusting in a different God, a different Christ, and a different way of salvation from the biblical God, Christ and way of salvation. All of your beliefs are based on the writings of Joseph Smith, who is proven to be a discredited prophet, not a prophet of God. Do you want to face the judgment and eternity trusting the Mormon gods, or the God of the Bible?

The Bible

"And Thomas answered and said unto him, (Jesus) My Lord and my God" (John 20:28).

"If thou shalt confess with thy mouth the Lord Jesus, and shalt believe in thine heart that God hath raised him from the dead, thou shalt be saved. For with the heart man believeth unto righteousness; and with the mouth confession is made unto salvation" (Rom. 10:9,10).

Mormon Writers

"As man is, God once was: as God is, man may be" (James E. Talmage, A Study of the *Articles of Faith,* published by The Church of Jesus Christ of Latter-day Saints, 1957, p. 430).

"Christ the Word, the Firstborn, had of course attained unto the status of Godhood while yet in pre-existence" (B. R. McConkie, *What the Mormons Think of Christ,* published by The Church of Jesus Christ of Latter-day Saints, p. 36).

"He [Adam] is our Father and our God and the only God with whom we have to do" (Brigham Young, *Journal of Discourses,* vol. 1, 1966, p. 50).

"The child Jesus... was not begotten of the Holy Ghost" (Brigham Young, *Journal of Discourses,* vol. 1, pp. 50, 51).

"For we know that it is by grace that we are saved, after all we can do" (Joseph Smith, *Book of Mormon* 2 Nephi 25:23).

Comment

The choice is clear, Mormonism or Christianity, *Joseph Smith or Jesus Christ.*

For additional information see chapters 7 and 13 in this book.

17. The Bible teaches instant and complete personal salvation through Jesus Christ. Mormons do not believe in instant and complete personal salvation. Which do you believe?

The Bible

"For whosoever shall *call* upon the name of the Lord shall be saved" (Rom. 10:13).

Mormon Writers

"Redemption from personal sins can only be obtained through obedience to the requirements of the Gospel, and a life of good works" (James E. Talmage, *Articles of Faith*, published by The Church of Jesus Christ of Latter-day Saints, 1952, pp. 85, 87).

Comment

How long does it take to *call*, to ask Christ to save you?

18. Would like to ask the biblical Lord Jesus Christ to save you right now? God loves you and wants you to be saved.

Here is *exactly* how you can be saved: Just pray if you mean it, the best you know how, with all your heart, "Lord Jesus Christ, come into my heart and life. Cleanse me from all sin by your shed blood. Make me a child of God. Give me your free gift of everlasting life, and let me *know* that I am saved now and forever. I now receive you as my very own personal Lord and Saviour. In Jesus name, Amen."

Did you mean this prayer? Then did Jesus save you? He promised that "Whosoever shall call upon the name of the Lord shall be saved" (Rom. 10:13). If you called believingly on Him, He had to save you or He lied. According to His Word He *cannot* lie! So, did He save you? You can *know* you are saved right now, not just according to your feeling, but because *God's Word says so*. To wait for feeling is to deny faith!

Now let's memorize John 3:36 together as we read it out loud three times: "He that believeth on the Son hath everlasting life." What do you have right now according to God's Word? If you were to die right now where would you go, according to God's Word? If you *know* that Jesus has saved you according to His Word, thank Him out loud for saving you!

The reality of your salvation will be shown in your love-response in obeying and following Jesus Christ. "If a man love me, he will keep my words" (John 14:23). If you are truly saved, you will obey Christ's command. Naturally, this includes coming out of Mormonism.

You will grow in assurance and in His love as you:

(1) Attend faithfully a church that believes in the Bible and the Bible *alone*, and that believes the blood of Jesus Christ *alone* can cleanse from sin!

(2) Confess Christ in public and be baptized.

(3) Pray daily.

(4) Read the Bible daily. Start with the Gospel of John.

(5) Share Christ with others.

(6) Confess your sin instantly.

(7) Let Jesus live His life through you.

(8) Turn away from anything that would hinder you from following Christ.

Comment

Real love cares enough to tell the truth. Jesus loves you, my Mormon friend, and so do I love you, enough to want you to be saved and be in heaven with me forever, loving and serving the Lord Jesus Christ together.

Floyd C. McElveen
Route 2, space 10
Burley, Idaho 83318

Bibliography

Budvarson, Arthur. *Book of Mormon—True or False?* Concord, Calif.: Pacific Pub. Co., 1959.

Cowan, Marvin W. *Mormon Claims Answered.* Published by Marvin W. Cowan, 1975.

Hunter, Milton R. *The Gospel Through the Ages.* Salt Lake City: Deseret Book Co., 1945.

McConkie, Bruce R. *Doctrines of Salvation.* Salt Lake City: Bookcraft, Inc., 1954.

———*Mormon Doctrine.* Salt Lake City: Bookcraft, Inc. 1966.

———*What the Mormons Think of Christ* (tract). Salt Lake City: Deseret News Press, no date.

McKay, David O. *Gospel Ideals.* Salt Lake City: The Church

of Jesus Christ of Latter-day Saints, 1953.

Nelson, Dee Jay. *The Joseph Smith Papyri, Part 2*. Salt Lake City, 1968.

Richards, LeGrand. *A Marvelous Work and a Wonder*. Salt Lake City: Deseret Book Co., 1950.

Richards, Stephen L. *Contributions of Joseph Smith*. Salt Lake City: The Church of Jesus Christ of Latter-day Saints.

Roberts, B. H. *A Comprehensive History of The Church of Jesus Christ of Latter-day Saints*. Salt Lake City: Deseret News Press, 1930.

Smith, Joseph, Jr. *The Book of Mormon*. Salt Lake City: The Church of Jesus Christ of Latter-day Saints.

————*Doctrine and Covenants*. Salt Lake City: The Church of Jesus Christ of Latter-day Saints.

————*Inspired Version of the Holy Scriptures*. Independence: Herald Pub. House, 1955.

————*The History of the Church of Jesus Christ of Latter-day Saints*. 6 vols. Salt Lake City: Deseret News, 1902–12.

————*The Pearl of Great Price*. Salt Lake City: The Church of Jesus Christ of Latter-day Saints, 1958.

Smith, Joseph Fielding, comp. *Teachings of Prophet Joseph Smith*. Salt Lake City: Deseret News Press, 1958.

Talmage, James E. A Study of the *Articles of Faith*. 36th ed. Salt Lake City: The Church of Jesus Christ of Latter-day Saints, 1957.

Tanner, Jerald. *Mormonism*: A Study of Mormon History and Doctrine. Clearfield, Utah: Utah Evangel Press, 1962.

Tanner, Jerald and Sandra. *The First Vision Examined*. Salt Lake City: Modern Microfilm Co., 1969.

————*Joseph Smith's 1826 Trial*. Salt Lake City: Modern Microfilm Co., 1971.

————*Mormonism—Shadow or Reality*. Salt Lake City: Modern Microfilm Co., 1975.

Turner, Wallace. *The Mormon Establishment*. Boston: Houghton Mifflin Co., 1966.

Widtsoe, John A. *Evidences and Reconciliations.* Salt Lake City: Bookcraft, Inc., 1969.

———*Joseph Smith—Seeker After Truth.* Salt Lake City: Bookcraft, Inc., 1951.

Whitmer, David. *An Address to All Believers in Christ.* Reprint; Searcy, Ark.: Bales Bookstore, 1960.

Wilson, Robert Dick. *A Scientific Investigation of the Old Testament.* Chicago: Moody Press.

In addition to the books named above I have been in contact with the following students in Mormonism who have assisted and encouraged me: Jim Bjornstad, Jerry Urban, Wesley P. Walters, Einar Anderson, and Wally Tope.